Nick Hornby

Slam

Teacher's Guide
von Miriam Bögel

Ernst Klett Sprachen
Stuttgart

Bildquellennachweis

Cover: shutterstock (Elanur us), New York, NY; **Seite 58**: Penguin Group (UK), London WC2R ORL; **Seite 61**: Trbune Media Services, Inc. All Rights Reserved. Reprinted with permission.; **Seite 80**: Ullstein Bild GmbH, Berlin; **Seite 80**: Interfoto (NG Collection), München; **Seiten 65, 66, 67, 68, 69**: Fotolia LLC (frenta), New York

Nicht in allen Fällen war es uns möglich, den Rechteinhaber der Abbildungen ausfindig zu machen. Berechtigte Ansprüche werden selbstverständlich im Rahmen der üblichen Vereinbarungen abgegolten.

1. Auflage   1 ⁶ ⁵ ⁴ ³ | 2016 15 14 13

Alle Drucke dieser Auflage sind unverändert und können im Unterricht nebeneinander verwendet werden.

Die letzte Zahl bezeichnet das Jahr des Druckes. Das Werk und seine Teile sind urheberrechtlich geschützt. Jede Nutzung in anderen als den gesetzlich zugelassenen Fällen bedarf der vorherigen schriftlichen Einwilligung des Verlags. Hinweis zu § 52 a UrhG: Weder das Werk noch seine Teile dürfen ohne eine solche Einwilligung eingescannt und in ein Netzwerk eingestellt werden. Dies gilt auch für Intranets von Schulen und sonstigen Bildungseinrichtungen. Fotomechanische oder andere Wiedergabeverfahren nur mit Genehmigung des Verlags.

Every attempt has been made to contact copyright holders. Additions or corrections to the names and/or organisations printed herein will be welcomed.

© Ernst Klett Sprachen GmbH, Rotebühlstraße 77, 70178 Stuttgart, 2010.
Alle Rechte vorbehalten.

Internetadresse: www.klett.de / www.lektueren.com

Autorin: Miriam Bögel
Redaktion: Jochen Lohmeyer
Layoutkonzeption: Elmar Feuerbach
Gestaltung und Satz: Satz & mehr, Starenweg 2, 74354 Besigheim
Umschlaggestaltung: Elmar Feuerbach
Druck und Bindung: Digitaldruck Tebben, Biessenhofen

Printed in Germany

ISBN 978-3-12-579823-6

Nick Hornby

Slam

Inhaltsverzeichnis

I. Einführung

Synopse 6

Historische, politische, sozio-kulturelle
Hintergründe 6

Angaben zum Autor 7

Eignung für Sek. I und Sek. II 8

Module und Zeitkontingente 8

Tabellarische Stundenübersicht 9

Kapitelübersicht des Romans 12

II. Module

Pre-reading activities (1 Stunde) 15

While-reading activities (16-19 Stunden) 16

Modul 1: Who are Sam and Alicia? (2 Stunden) ... 16

Modul 2: Sam and Alicia in love (3-4 Stunden) 19

Modul 3: Alicia's pregnancy (3-4 Stunden) 24

Modul 4: Learning to cope with pregnancy
(1 Stunde) 32

Modul 5: Preventing teenage pregnancy
(4-5 Stunden) 34

Modul 6: Wrapping up the novel (3 Stunden) 40

Post-reading activities (6-15 Stunden) 44

Modul 7: Film analysis *Juno* (5-6 Stunden) 44

Modul 8: Creating a film trailer for *Slam*
(4 Stunden) 50

Modul 9: Ideensammlung weiterer *activities* 53

Klausuren: Lösungen 54

III. Anhang

Kopiervorlagen 58

Klausuren 89

I. Einführung

Synopse

Der fünfzehnjährige Skater Sam ist einmal kurz unvorsichtig beim Sex mit seiner Freundin Alicia, gerade als die beiden langsam das Interesse aneinander verlieren. Es kommt wie es kommen muss: Alicia wird schwanger und zu Sams Unglück beschließt sie, das Kind zu behalten. Da Sam selbst das Resultat einer Teenager-Schwangerschaft ist und seine inzwischen geschiedenen Eltern ihm unaufhörlich erklären, wie sehr die junge Elternschaft beider Leben beeinträchtigt hat, wendet sich Sam an seinen Helden, den Profi-Skater Tony Hawk, oder vielmehr Tonys Poster, und fragt ihn um Rat. Die Antworten, die Tony gibt – zumindest bildet sich Sam ein, diese zu hören – stammen alle aus Hawks Biographie, die Sam diverse Male gelesen hat und die er inzwischen auswendig kennt. Oft klingen die Antworten aufgrund dieser Umstände recht kryptisch, doch Sam hört aus ihnen heraus, was er hören möchte. Seine Ängste bezüglich seiner zukünftigen Rolle als minderjähriger Vater kann Tony ihm jedoch nicht nehmen, so dass Sam in einer Kurzschlusshandlung von Zuhause wegrennt. Er erkennt jedoch recht schnell, dass er ohne Geld, ohne Schulabschluss und ohne seine Freunde und Familie ein Leben führen müsste, das in keiner Weise besser ist als das, was ihn zu Hause erwartet, weshalb er bereits nach einem Tag wieder zurückkehrt, um sich seiner Verantwortung zu stellen. Immer noch voller Zukunftsangst wird er auf magische Art und Weise eines Nachts in die Zukunft transportiert, wo er einen kurzen Ausschnitt seines zukünftigen Lebens sehen kann. Obwohl er dadurch immer noch nicht für die frühe Vaterschaft bereit ist, erkennt er, dass er die Situation in den Griff bekommen wird und dass sein Leben nicht so zerstört sein wird, wie er es sich vorstellt.

Historische, politische, sozio-kulturelle Hintergründe

Großbritannien hat seit Jahren die höchste Teenager Schwangerschaftsrate in Europa. Nach Veröffentlichung der erschreckend hohen Zahlen für das Jahr 1998 – 4,7% der Mädchen zwischen 15 und 17 wurden in dem Jahr schwanger – entwickelte die Regierung eine Millionen Pfund teure Kampagne, um die Ursachen aber auch die Konsequenzen von Teenager Schwangerschaften zu bekämpfen. Konkret hat die *Teenage Pregnancy Strategy* zwei Ziele: Bis 2010 soll die Empfängnisrate bei den unter-18-Jährigen halbiert sowie ein deutlicher Abwärtstrend in der Altersgruppe der unter-16-Jährigen etabliert werden, gleichzeitig soll die Quote der jugendlichen Eltern in schulischer und beruflicher Ausbildung sowie in Beschäftigung bis 2010 auf 60% erhöht werden, um deren Risiko der sozialen Ausgrenzung zu reduzieren. Diese Ziele sollen durch konzertierte Aktionen verschiedener Organisationen, nationalen Medienkampagnen, Unterstützung der Eltern von Teenagern, Prävention im Sinne einer verbesserten Sexualerziehung in Schulen und erleichterten Zugang zu Verhütungsmitteln sowie Unterstützung von Teenager Eltern erreicht werden.

Das Büro für Nationale Statistik enthüllte jedoch mit der Veröffentlichung der Zahlen für 2005 einen Zuwachs von 281 Schwangerschaften in der Altersgruppe der unter-16-Jährigen im Vergleich zum Vorjahr sowie den größten jährlichen Anstieg in der Altersgruppe der unter-18-Jährigen in 10 Jahren. Die Regierung bestätigte daraufhin, dass die gesetzten Ziele für 2010 kaum zu erreichen sind und beschuldigte gleichzeitig die Eltern der Teenager, keine Hilfe in der Reduzierung der Schwangerschaftsraten zu sein. Dies ist aus Sicht der Kritiker der Kampagne bloße Ironie, da im Rahmen der Kampagne Abtreibungen und Empfängnisverhütung ohne Kenntnis der Eltern nun ohne Altersbeschränkungen möglich sind. Ebenso haben die Jugendlichen freien und kostenlosen Zugang zur „Pille danach", was aber bisher keine positive Wirkung gezeigt hat. Dass seit Beginn der Kampagne die Zahl der Infektionen mit Geschlechtskrankheiten unter Jugendlichen dramatisch gestiegen ist, zeigt eher, dass die Kampagne ihre Wirkung nicht nur verfehlt, sondern scheinbar Jugendliche vielmehr zum sexuellen Experimentieren einlädt.

Angaben zum Autor

Nick Hornby wurde am 17. April 1957 in Redhill/Surrey (England) geboren. Er selbst schreibt auf seiner Homepage, dass er seine Ausbildung an der Cambridge University, wo er Englisch studierte, und in Highbury, North London, seinem heutigen Wohnort, durchlief, wo er alles über Fußball und die Fakten des Lebens lernte. Im Laufe der Jahre arbeitete Hornby als Englischlehrer u.a. für Englisch als Fremdsprache, betreute Samsung Führungskräfte, die zu Besuch in England waren, und wurde dann Journalist und Popmusik-Kritiker für die Zeitschrift *New Yorker*. Schon während seines Studiums schrieb Hornby Theaterstücke, die er selbst als schlecht bezeichnet, da ihm zum Schreiben gelungener Dialoge die passende Stimme fehlte. Erst als er Werke der amerikanischen Autoren Anne Tyler, Raymond Carver, Richard Ford und Lorrie Moore gelesen hatte, hatte er diese Stimme der Einfachheit, voller Humor und Seele gefunden, die seiner Meinung nach in der britischen Literatur bis dahin fehlte.

Hornbys Erstlingswerk war eine Sammlung kritischer Essays über amerikanische Autoren, danach folgten internationale Bestseller wie *High Fidelity*, *About a Boy*, *How To Be Good*, *A Long Way Down*, *Fever Pitch* und *Slam*, Hornbys erster Jugendroman. *Fever Pitch*, *High Fidelity* und *About a Boy* wurden bereits erfolgreich mit Stars wie Hugh Grant, Colin Firth, Drew Barrymore und John Cusack verfilmt, Johnny Depp produzierte den Film zu *A Long Way Down*. Außerdem ist Hornby Mitbegründer des *Treehouse Trust*, einer Wohltätigkeitsorganisation, die eine Schule für autistische Kinder unterstützt, zu der auch Hornbys Sohn Danny geht. Die Erlöse der Kurzgeschichtensammlung *Speaking with the Angel*, mit Hornby als Mitautor und Herausgeber, kommen der Schule zugute. Darüber hinaus gewann Hornby für seine Werke verschiedene Preise, u.a. den *WH Smith Book Award*, bei dem die Leser ihre Stimmen abgeben, oder den *Writers' Writer Award*, verliehen von namhaften Autoren wie Germaine Greer, Zadie Smith und Doris Lessing.

Über *Slam* sagt Hornby[1], er habe den Roman nicht speziell für eine jugendliche Leserschaft geschrieben, nur weil der Protagonist ein Jugendlicher ist. Er habe zwar mit seinem Verleger besprochen, irgendwann einmal einen Jugendroman zu schreiben, Anlass für *Slam* war jedoch die Beobachtung eines Teenager

---

1   vgl. Interview mit Nick Hornby im Anhang der Klett-Textausgabe (ISBN 978-3-12-579822-9)

Elternpaares und die Erkenntnis, dass von Teenager-Schwangerschaften nicht nur Mädchen betroffen sind. Aus dem Nachdenken über den jungen Vater wurde dann die Idee für den Roman geboren und obwohl die Rate an Teenager-Schwangerschaften in Großbritannien höher ist als in allen anderen Ländern Europas, will Hornby mit seinem Roman nicht belehren. Anders als der aktuelle Trend in zeitgenössischer Literatur, ist es ihm jedoch wichtig, dass seine Charaktere an irgendeiner Stelle des Romans das Richtige tun und nicht unrettbar, hoffnungslos und verloren sind, und Sam tut dies offensichtlich, als er sich dazu entscheidet, Verantwortung für sein Kind zu übernehmen.

Eignung für Sek. I und Sek. II

Auf der sprachlichen Ebene bietet sich der Einsatz des Romans im Englischunterricht je nach dem Leistungsstand der Lerngruppe ab der 9. Klasse an. Es hat sich gezeigt, dass auch Schülerinnen und Schüler mit Englisch als zweiter Fremdsprache sich am Ende dieser Jahrgangsstufe sehr schnell in den Roman einlesen und auch die zahlreich vorkommenden umgangssprachlichen Ausdrücke gut verstehen. Aufgrund der brisanten, jedoch sehr schülernahen Thematik des Romans empfiehlt sich der Einsatz insbesondere in den Jahrgangsstufen 9 bis 11, da Sam und Alicia ein hohes Identifikationspotential für die 15- bis 17-Jährigen bieten. Neben interkultureller Kompetenz schult der Einsatz eines originalsprachlichen Romans insbesondere die Lesekompetenz der Schülerinnen und Schüler. Das Thema *Growing up*, das in den Jahrgangsstufen 9 bis 11 in allen deutschen Lehrplänen auftaucht, wird intensiv behandelt, wobei die Probleme des Heranwachsens einschließlich seiner negativen Erfahrungen, aber auch der ersten Liebe des Protagonisten im Zentrum stehen.

Module und Zeitkontingente

Der *Teacher's Guide* ist im Modulverfahren basierend auf dem klassischen hierarchisch gegliederten Unterrichtsplan mit *pre-*, *while-* und *post-reading activities* aufgebaut. Zwar bauen die Module 1 bis 6 aufeinander auf, es ist jedoch durchaus möglich, die einzelnen Themen individuell zu kürzen und nur einen Teil der Kopiervorlagen einzusetzen. Man sollte jedoch dabei bedenken, dass Schülerinnen und Schüler der Jahrgangsstufen 9 bis 11 ihre Lesekompetenz besonders im Bereich der Fremdsprachen noch ausbilden müssen und ein zu großes Pensum an Leseaufträgen bzw. ein zu schnelles Vorgehen eher zu Lesefrustration als zum Lesegenuss führen können. Die Behandlung der *post-reading activities* ist fakultativ und sollte sich an der Motivation der Lernenden – manchmal ist zu einem Thema einfach genug gesagt worden – und der zur Verfügung stehenden Zeit orientieren. Auch die Klausuren können als *post-reading activities* eingesetzt werden. Insgesamt sollten mindestens 20 Unterrichtsstunden für den Einsatz des Romans eingeplant werden.

Stundenübersicht

Pre-reading activities (1 Std.)

Dauer	Kapitel	Unterrichtsinhalt/ Ziel	Unterrichtsgegenstand	Unterrichtsmethode
1	1	**Einstieg** zur Lesemotivation anhand des Umschlags der Erstausgabe.	**KV 1.1** *The cover* **KV 1.2** *The blurb*	EA, PA, UG

While-reading activities (16-19 Std.)

Modul 1				
2	1-2	**Who is Sam?** Erste Charakterisierung des Protagonisten und Anlegen eines *character file* für Alicia.	**KV 2** *Sam's character file*	EA, UG, Partnerpuzzle
Modul 2				
3-4	3-5	**Sam and Alicia in love** Sich mit dem Thema Liebe auseinandersetzen und einen Bezug zum Roman herstellen.	**KV 3** *Love is…* **KV 4** *Love?* **KV 5** *Vocabulary "Dating and love"*	EA, UG, Meinungsbarometer, Kugellager, Schneeballsystem
Modul 3				
3-4	5-9	**Alicia's pregnancy** Wortschatzerwerb zu den Wortfeldern *Alicia's feelings* und *sex, pregnancy and birth*. Die Konsequenzen einer Teenager-Schwangerschaft erkennen.	**KV 6** *Sex, pregnancy and birth* **KV 7.1-7.5** *There are choices to make* **KV 8** *The parents' reactions*	EA, GA, UG, Folien-Präsentation der Flussdiagramme, Rollenspiel *Good angel/ bad angel*, Innerer Monolog
Modul 4				
1 (1-2)	10-12 (13-20)	**Learning to cope with pregnancy** Die Inhalte der Kapitel 10-12 wiedergeben und den Zweck der Zukunftsvisionen Sams erkennen.	**KV 9** *Learning to cope with pregnancy* **KV 10** *Ideas for checking reading comprehension*	EA, UG
Modul 5				
4-5		**Preventing teenage pregnancy** Das Ausmaß der Problematik in GB erkennen, verschiedene Medienkampagnen kennenlernen und bewerten.	**KV 11** *Preventing teenage pregnancy* **KV 12** *Working with tables, graphs and charts* – Statistiken im Anhang der Textausgabe **KV 13** *British national media campaigns* **KV 14** *Evaluating a presentation* **KV 15** *Preparing a talk show* **KV 16** *Useful discussion phrases and tips*	Think-Pair-Share, PA, GA, Präsentationen, Talk Show

I. Einführung

Dauer	Kapitel	Unterrichtsinhalt/ Ziel	Unterrichtsgegenstand	Unterrichtsmethode
Modul 6				
3	13-20	**Wrapping up the novel** Wichtige Kernpunkte am Ende der Lektüre erkennen und auswerten.	Interview mit Nick Hornby im Anhang der Textausgabe **KV 17** *Writing a book review*	UG, Stummes Schreibgespräch Buchpräsentation

Post-reading activities

Dauer	Kapitel	Unterrichtsinhalt/ Ziel	Unterrichtsgegenstand	Unterrichtsmethode
Modul 7				
5-6	alle	**Juno** Eine Teenager-Schwangerschaft aus der Sicht der Mutter kennenlernen und mit der Sicht des Vaters in *Slam* vergleichen.	**KV 18** *Film posters of the film"Juno"* **KV 19.1-19.3** *Film dialogues* **KV 20** *Film review – "Juno"*	UG, Bildbeschreibung, Mediation
Modul 8				
4	alle	**Creating a film trailer for *Slam*** Die Schlüsselszenen aus *Slam* bestimmen, Kenntnisse der Filmgestaltung gewinnen und anwenden.	**KV 21.1-21.2** *Film terms: camera shots, angles and movements* **KV 22** *Camera work* **KV 23** *Creating your own storyboard*	EA, PA, GA, Gestalten eines Trailers zu *Slam*
Modul 9				
varia-bel		**Ideensammlung weiterer *activities***		• Soundtrack zum Roman gestalten • Designen eines neuen Covers • Präsentationen (Skating, Tony Hawk, Teenage pregnancy in the USA) • Eggbert: Sich um ein "Baby"kümmern • Spielen der Lieblingsszenen • Brief an Nick Hornby
		Klausuren	Klausur A Klausur B Klausur C	Vergleich mit einem Song und Zeitungsartikeln

Literatur

Hornby, Nick, *Slam*, Ernst Klett Sprachen, Stuttgart 2009.

Hornby, Nick, *Slam*, Penguin audio book, London 2007.

Haß, Frank (Hrsg.), *Fachdidaktik Englisch – Tradition, Innovation, Praxis*, Ernst Klett Sprachen, Stuttgart 2006.

Hesse/Putjenter, *Teacher's Guide zu „Dear Nobody"*, Ernst Klett Sprachen, Stuttgart 2000.

Juno, Twentieth Century Fox Home Entertainment, 2008.

www.candi.ac.uk/about/news/2006-7/news_%E2%80%9Cwant_respect_wear_a_co.aspx (Kampagne zur Reduzierung von Teenager Schwangerschaften)

www.munichx.de (Filmkritik zu *Juno*)

www.ottawacitizen.com/Health/Teen+pregnancy+target+YouTube+ploy/1621625/story.html (Zeitungsartikel und Videolink über ein Video zur Abschreckung vor Teenager Schwangerschaften)

www.parentlineplus.org.uk/index.php?id=784 (Kampagne zur Reduzierung von Teenager Schwangerschaften)

www.penguin.co.uk/static/cs/uk/0/minisites/nickhornby/index.html (Nick Hornbys offizielle Homepage)

www.ruthinking.co.uk (Kampagne zur Reduzierung von Teenager Schwangerschaften)

www.spinebreakers.co.uk/Creative/Pages/gedged.aspx (Poster-Wettbewerb zu *Slam*)

www.statistics.gov.uk/hub/search/index.html?newquery=teen+pregnancy (Office for National Statistics)

www.teenchoices.com/ (amerikanische Kampagne zur Reduzierung von Teenager Schwangerschaften)

www.theatlantic.com/doc/200711u/nick-hornby-interview (Interview mit Nick Hornby)

www.thenationalcampaign.org (The National Campaign to Prevent Teen and Unplanned Pregnancy)

www.thesun.co.uk/sol/homepage/news/article2233878.ece (Zeitungsartikel über den 12jährigen Vater Alfie Patten)

www.tonyhawk.com/bio.html (Tony Hawks offizielle Homepage)

www.youtube.com/watch?v=0VpX4ZWDviM&feature=related (Kampagne zur Reduzierung von Teenager Schwangerschaften)

www.youtube.com/watch?v=gGrp2ppsIgo (Kampagne zur Reduzierung von Teenager Schwangerschaften)

www.youtube.com/watch?v=Hn6mIK8G2Vc (amerikanische Kampagne zur Reduzierung von Teenager Schwangerschaften)

www.youtube.com/watch?v=K0SKf0K3bxg (*Juno*-Trailer)

I.   Einführung

Kapitelübersicht des Romans

Chapter	Pages	Summary
1	9-15	Sam introduces himself and his family situation. He also explains why he is talking to a poster of Tony Hawk.
2	16-46	Sam accompanies his mother to her colleague's birthday party. He meets Alicia and is fascinated by her even though she treats him badly at the beginning. They go out on a date the following evening but instead of watching a movie they go back to Alicia's house and have sex for the first time.
3	47-59	Sam describes how much he is in love with Alicia. His mother thinks that meeting Alicia every day is not healthy and wants to have one evening with Sam alone. They go out for pizza and a movie. The next day Sam and Alicia are more than happy to see each other again. They have sex without using a condom initially. Another evening Alicia is invited to Sam's house because his mum wants to meet her.
4	60-69	Sam gets bored with Alicia and starts living his old life again. When he is invited to a family lunch with Alicia's brother, their parents talk to him in a condescending manner, believing he is not very bright and didn't have the same opportunities. Sam's mum has a date with Mark. Sam breaks up with Alicia by not answering her text messages and not seeing her anymore.
5	70-80	The evening before his sixteenth birthday, Sam has a date with a girl from school who tells him she would like to have a baby. Sam decides not even to kiss her, let alone have sex with anybody ever again. The next morning he receives a text message from Alicia, who needs to see him urgently. She tells him that her period is three weeks late and while she is getting money for a pregnancy test, Sam leaves and switches off his mobile phone. Besides, he has lost his confidence in TH.
6	81-99	Sam thinks he is whizzed into the future by Tony Hawk: He and Alicia have a baby boy called Roof – a name Sam does not like at all. They live together in Alicia's room and Sam, not having learned how to cope with a baby, feels insecure when he has to take care of his son. He finds out his mother is pregnant, too. The next morning he wakes up back in his room again, regretting that he has ever had sex with Alicia.
7	100-111	Sam panics, takes his last 40 pounds and runs away to Hastings, the only place he has ever been to outside London. There he unsuccessfully tries to find a job in the arcades at the sea front. In the Bed & Breakfast he wants to spend the night he meets a grumpy old man who hires Sam as a helper.
8	112-122	The old man treats Sam badly and calls him stupid which makes him finally realize that running away from home was a mistake. He returns to London where he finds out that his mother has already called the police. As an explanation for his running away he mentions, among other things, his parents' divorce. Out of guilt his mum wants to arrange an appointment with a counsellor. Sam sneaks around outside Alicia's house but avoids knocking and finding out whether she is pregnant or not.
9	123-148	Three days later Alicia knocks on his door and confirms her pregnancy. She has already decided to keep the baby but is scared to talk to her parents. Sam realizes he misses talking to TH. In the afternoon Sam and his parents have a counselling session and his father soon finds out that not their divorce ten years earlier but Alicia is the problem. He even suspects that Sam "has knocked her up" but Sam keeps quiet. The following day they first tell Alicia's parents and later on Sam's mum about the pregnancy. The adults are upset and worry about their children's future.

10	149-160	Sam's report of the next few weeks: − His mum tells his father about the pregnancy. He takes it with good humour. − They find out about it at school and surprisingly even the teachers are interested as they want to try out a new programme for teenage parents. − Sam and Alicia go to a scan and find out the baby is a boy. − They kiss on the way home and decide to get back together, but don't have a sexual relationship anymore. − They go to a maternity class and feel out of place because the other parents-to-be are much older. − Mark moves in with Sam and his mother.
11	161-168	Alicia's parents think that Sam has destroyed their daughter's life but they make an effort to be nice. They are surprised that Sam and Alicia want to live together in their house when the baby is born but accept this. Sam goes skating for the first time in weeks and realizes how perfect his life was before. Sam's mother tries to talk him out of moving in with Alicia but he shows responsibility.
12	169-182	Sam is whizzed into the future again: He does not live with Alicia anymore and he has a little baby sister. When he has to take Roof to the doctor's to get an injection, he makes a mess of the situation because he does not know his son's proper name. He spends the afternoon with his son and realizes he is looking forward to meeting him in reality. His mother confirms that Sam is doing alright and has not messed up his life completely.
13	183-190	Sam has a skating accident and his mother tells him to quit skating because he will have to be there for Alicia and the baby but he doesn't give it up. Some days later she tells him that she also is pregnant but Sam is not surprised. He says it is alright with him. Sam and Alicia take their final exams, Sam enrols for sixth form college, Alicia takes a year off for the baby.
14	191-206	Alicia gives birth to the baby while her mother and Sam are present. Instead of the teenagers' CDs prepared for that occasion they listen to a singer Alicia's mum likes: Rufus Wainwright. Alicia decides to call her child Rufus Jones. Rufus after the singer, Jones like Sam's last name.
15	207-210	Sam moves in with Alicia the next day. He brings his TH poster along but hides it under the bed because he is embarrassed to admit he sometimes talks to the poster.
16	211-222	Sam lives through the first night TH whizzed him into and finds that the future is not as terrible as it looked at first. At college Sam fights with another boy who claims to be Roof's father. Sam assumes that he is the boy Alicia had gone out with before she got together with Sam and that the boy might be right and Alicia just needed a father for her child because the other boy broke up with her. He criticizes her and she proves him wrong. Nevertheless they argue.
17	223-231	They keep arguing the next days and weeks and after Sam's dad has taken him out for a drink one day to give him some parental advice – like they shouldn't try to make their relationship last longer than it is worth it – he leaves, pretending it to be only for a few days because of a bad cold.
18	232-237	Sam finds information about teenage pregnancies on the internet and is shocked about the statistics that say 80% of teenage fathers lose touch with their kids completely. He immediately goes to Alicia to tell her that this won't happen to them but has a row with her instead. Alicia's mum suggests numerous scenarios why he could lose touch with Roof but Sam decides to make the best effort he can.

19	238-250	Sam answers questions the readers might ask from a point of view two years later: - His baby sister is born and everything is fine with his mum and Mark. - The day when he had to take Roof for his injection really happened but he didn't mess things up. - He had sex with Alicia once more and she thought that they were together again. - He thinks he is doing quite well with being a father and going to college but he is not really happy with his life.
20	251-254	Sam is whizzed into the future again: He has a new girlfriend and they meet Alicia and her new boyfriend. They all get along well and Sam learns that his life will be alright.

II. Module

Pre-reading activities (1 Std.)

Lernziel
Lesemotivation erzielen und Interesse am Hauptcharakter Sam und dessen Schicksal wecken.

Methode
Zur Einstimmung auf die Lektüre arbeiten die Schülerinnen und Schüler arbeitsteilig mit dem Original-Cover bzw. dem Klappentext des Romans. Beides steht in den Kopiervorlagen als Arbeitsblatt zur Verfügung (siehe **KV 1.1** und **KV 1.2**). Die Klasse wird in zwei Gruppen eingeteilt, die jeweils Vorhersagen machen oder Fragen über den Plot des Romans formulieren. Gruppe 1 arbeitet dabei mit dem Cover des Romans (**KV 1.1**), Gruppe 2 mit dem Klappentext (**KV 1.2**). Angeleitet durch die *useful phrases* machen alle Lernenden Notizen.

In einem zweiten Schritt vergleichen beide Gruppen ihre Ergebnisse in Partnerarbeit oder im Unterrichtsgespräch. Anschließend machen die Schülerinnen und Schüler weitere Vorhersagen auf der Grundlage der gewonnenen Informationen bezüglich der Charaktere, des "Unfalls", der im Klappentext erwähnt wird etc.

Die Ergebnisse können von einem Schüler auf ein Plakat übertragen werden, das im Klassenraum bis zum Ende der Unterrichtseinheit aufgehängt wird. Dies kann im Laufe des Leseprozesses ergänzt oder darauf Bezug genommen werden. Die anderen Schülerinnen und Schüler schreiben währenddessen ihre Vorhersagen in ihr Heft.

Fragestellung
What does the cover or blurb tell you about this book?

Ergebnis
Group 1:
The cover shows graffiti or a scribble containing
- the title and author of the book, a big flying heart with a banner displaying the name Alicia, several smaller hearts, the names Nick, Sam, Alicia and Tony, skateboards, birds, trainers, helmets and protectors, skaters, skulls, (probably) spray paint.

Group 2:
- hero of story is called Sam, sixteen years old, hobby: skateboarding, at the beginning of the story he ist happy, he makes a mistake and has to face the consequences.

Hausaufgabe
Write a paragraph each:
a) What will the novel be about? Are there any questions you might want to ask about the book?
b) Will you enjoy reading the book? Why (not)?

While-reading activities (16-19 Std.)

Die im Folgenden beschriebenen Unterrichtsstunden bauen aufeinander auf und unterstützen und begleiten den Leseprozess der Schülerinnen und Schüler. Ergänzungen seitens der Lehrkraft sind natürlich jederzeit möglich.

Modul 1   Who are Sam and Alicia? (2 Stunden)

Lernziel
Erste Charakterisierung der Hauptpersonen Sam und Alicia, sowie kennen lernen ihrer Lebensumstände.

Methode
Das erste Kapitel des Romans wird von einem lesestarken Lerngruppenmitglied oder der Lehrperson vorgelesen. Es kann ebenso von der Hörbuchversion vorgespielt werden (Penguin audio book, ISBN 978-0-141-80791-1). Im Anschluss sammeln die Schülerinnen und Schüler Fakten über Sams Leben und seinen Charakter mithilfe von **KV 2**.

Alternativ kann die Frage „What do we know about Sam after the first chapter?" auch ohne **KV 2** and die Lerngruppe gestellt werden. Die Antworten werden dann in einem klassischen Brainstorming mit *Clustering* vom Lehrer oder guten Schülerinnen und Schülern gesammelt. Die Vorstrukturierung fördert jedoch die *Scanning*-Fähigkeiten, das genaue Lesen und Erarbeiten von bestimmten Details, während beim offeneren Brainstorming die *Skimming*-Fähigkeiten, das schnelle Überfliegen eines Textes zur Entnahme der Hauptinformationen, geschult werden.

Fragestellung
What do we know about Sam after the first chapter?

Ergebnis
Name: Sam Jones

Age: 15, nearly 16

Family situation:
- mum and dad are divorced
- before the divorce they were fighting all the time
- now mum is working
- she has recently split up with her boyfriend Steve who Sam did not like
- obviously Sam is living with his mother

School performance:
- art and design is his best subject
- his performance is not so good in the other subjects
- he hates maths

Leisure time activities:
- skating = skateboarding
- has just learned 2 new tricks
- spends most of his time at Grind City

II. Modul 1

Idols:
- Tony Hawk = TH = The Birdman, who is the best skateboarder in the world
- has read TH's biography "Hawk – Occupation: Skateboarder" about 40 or 50 times
- has a poster of TH in his room to which he talks and which talks back, mainly in the form of quotations from the biography

Thoughts about life: life is good for the first time because in the past things have gone wrong

Additional information: he likes Alicia

(Haus-)Aufgaben
Read chapter 2 and

Group A: add information to Sam's character file.
or
Group B: start a character file for Alicia and put the information from the chapter into suitable categories.

Methode
Die Klasse wird für die (Haus-)Aufgabe in zwei Gruppen eingeteilt. Da Aufgabe für Gruppe B aufgrund der selbst zu findenden Kategorien etwas anspruchsvoller ist, empfiehlt sich ein binnendifferenziertes Vorgehen. Dabei sollten für die weitere Verarbeitung der Informationen (in der folgenden Stunde) jedoch beide Gruppen etwa gleich groß sein.

Die Verarbeitung der arbeitsteilig gewonnen Informationen erfolgt im Partnerpuzzle. Dazu tragen sich jeweils zwei SuS mit unterschiedlichen Arbeitsaufträgen ihre Ergebnisse vor. Der zuhörende Partner macht sich dabei Notizen.

Alternative: Alle Schülerinnen und Schüler bearbeiten Aufgabenteil A und vergleichen ihre Ergebnisse. Im Anschluss wird anstelle eines *character file* Alicias Profil im ,SchülerVZ' (oder z.B. für ,facebook.com') erstellt. Hierzu müssen die Schülerinnen und Schüler einen Perspektivenwechsel vornehmen und über die bloße Informationsentnahme hinaus überlegen, wie sich Alicia auf einer Internetplattform wie ,SchülerVZ' (Internet-Plattform mit einem Schülerverzeichnis) oder ,Facebook' präsentieren würde. Mit hoher Wahrscheinlichkeit kennen sich die Schülerinnen und Schüler im ,SchülerVZ' bestens aus und benötigen keine Anleitung, was hier erwartet wird. Da man für den Zugang im ,SchülerVZ' eine Einladung benötigt, kann sich die Lehrperson z.B. auf www.facebook.com über den Aufbau eines solchen Profils informieren.

Fragestellung

What do we know about Sam and Alicia after the second chapter?

Ergebnis

Gruppe A

Family situation:
- Sam's mum is 32 years old
- she works for Hackney council
- she was married at 16 because she was pregnant with Sam
- she wanted to study at university
- Sam's grandfather wanted to be a footballer and was offered a place at Queen's Park Rangers, so he dropped out of school
- in Sam's family people don't have interesting professional careers

School performance:
- school means a lot to Sam because he wants to be the first person in the family to get a qualification while being at school

Idols:
- Tony Hawk turned pro at the age of 14
- he lost his virginity at 16

Additional information:
- Alicia is his girlfriend now
- other friends are Rabbit and Rubbish
- Rabbit is stupid but a good skater
- he likes Sam's mum
- Rabbit's philosophy: Pain can't kill you
- Rubbish is a bad skater but nice to talk to

Gruppe B

Name: Alicia Burns

Age: 15, but she seems older than Sam

Outward appearance:
- Alicia is gorgeous with enormous grey eyes, messy and straw-coloured hair, the skin of a peach, and she is tall but not skinny or flat-chested

Character traits:
- she treats people badly (Sam describes her as arrogant, sharp and spiky; sulky and cocky) because they let her as she is pretty and gets away with it

Family situation:
- her mother is the councillor Sam's mother works for
- Sam and Alicia meet at her mother's fiftieth birthday party
- her brother is 19 and studies music at college
- her father teaches at university

II.   Modul 2

Love and relationships:
- Alicia is Sam's first love (he did not really see his previous girlfriends at all or the relationships lasted less than seven weeks)
- she asks Sam out to the cinema
- she split up with her boyfriend of two months because he wanted sex and she didn't
- she has sex with Sam after their first date

School performance:
- Alicia does not go to the same school as Sam
- she is not too good at school and does not want to go to college
- she wants to be a model

Additional information:
- she likes hip-hop music and REM
- she plays the piano
- she lives in a big, old house with many books

(Haus-)Aufgaben

Die folgende Aufgabe ist zeitaufwändig und sollte daher als Hausaufgabe gestellt werden. Die Auswertung erfolgt weiter unten.

Read chapter 3 and start listing arguments that might help answer the question "Is this love (between Sam and Alicia)?".

Modul 2   Sam and Alicia in love (3-4 Stunden)

Lernziel

Sich mit dem Thema Liebe und dessen Bedeutung auseinandersetzen und einen Bezug zum Roman herstellen.

Methode

Als Einstieg ins Thema (der sich aufgrund des weiteren Vorgehens nicht unbedingt zu Beginn einer Unterrichtsstunde anbietet) bearbeiten die Schülerinnen und Schüler **KV 3**. Hierbei soll jeder anhand der *Love is…* – Cartoons eine passende Bildunterschrift und damit eine Aussage zum Thema Liebe finden, die z.T. sehr persönlich sein kann. Da möglicherweise Hemmungen bestehen, die Ergebnisse vorzutragen, kann die Lehrperson die ausgefüllten Arbeitsblätter einsammeln und selbst vortragen oder bunt gemischt wieder austeilen und von den Schülerinnen und Schülern vortragen lassen. Im Anschluss kann diskutiert (und evtl. abgestimmt) werden, welche Aussage die Lernenden am treffendsten finden.

Fragestellung

What is, in your opinion, a good definition of love?

Ergebnis

Die Schülerinnen und Schüler gewinnen einen Eindruck von der Vielfältigkeit der Auffassungen darüber, was Liebe ist. Die tatsächliche Bildunterschrift lautet: „… discovering the more you see of someone, the more you see in someone." Diese

19

II. Modul 2

Lösung kann von den Schülerinnen und Schülern natürlich nicht erwartet werden, allerdings werden die Lernenden üblicherweise diese Information einfordern.

(Haus-)Aufgabe

Read chapter 3 and start listing arguments that might help answer the question "Would you call the feelings that Sam and Alicia have for each other 'love'?"

<u>Hinweis:</u> Die Auswertung dieser Aufgabe erfolgt nicht gleich im nächsten Unterrichtsschritt.

Methode

Als Einstieg in die nächste Stunde sammeln die Schülerinnen und Schüler Sprichwörter und Redewendungen über Liebe und Sex, die von der Lehrkraft an der Tafel gesammelt werden. Eine Auswahl an Möglichkeiten findet man in **KV 4**, die den Lernenden als Folie präsentiert werden kann. Alternativ kann die Lehrperson die Sprichwörter über Liebe in ähnlicher Form an der Tafel notieren, so dass die Sammlung der Lerngruppe direkt zum Einsatz kommt.

Auf der Folie bzw. an der Tafel sollen die Positionen von Sam und Alicia bezüglich der gesammelten Sprichwörter diskutiert und mit unterschiedlichen Symbolen markiert werden. Um alle Schülerinnen und Schüler an der Positionsfindung zu beteiligen, kann ein sogenanntes Meinungsbarometer eingesetzt werden. Dazu hängt die Lehrperson an einem Ende des Klassenraums ein DIN A3 Blatt beschriftet mit „agree", am anderen Ende ein Blatt mit der Beschriftung „disagree" auf. Nacheinander werden die Aussagen vorgelesen und die Schülerinnen und Schüler nehmen in der Rolle von Sam bzw. Alicia eine Position zwischen „agree" und „disagree" ein. Nun kann der Lehrer einzelne Personen befragen, mit welcher Begründung sie an dieser Stelle stehen. Die Nähe zu „agree" bzw. „disagree" gibt dabei den Grad der Zustimmung oder Ablehnung an. Bei Konsensfindung wird das entsprechende Symbol auf der Folie bzw. der Tafel gesetzt. Bei entsprechender Klassengröße ist es ebenfalls denkbar, die Klasse zu teilen, so dass die eine Hälfte jeweils Alicias Position, die andere Hälfte Sams Position einnimmt.

Fragestellungen

What are popular sayings and beliefs about love and sex?

What would Sam and Alicia think about these?

Ergebnis

Ein mögliches Ergebnis, jedoch ohne Begründung, könnte so aussehen:

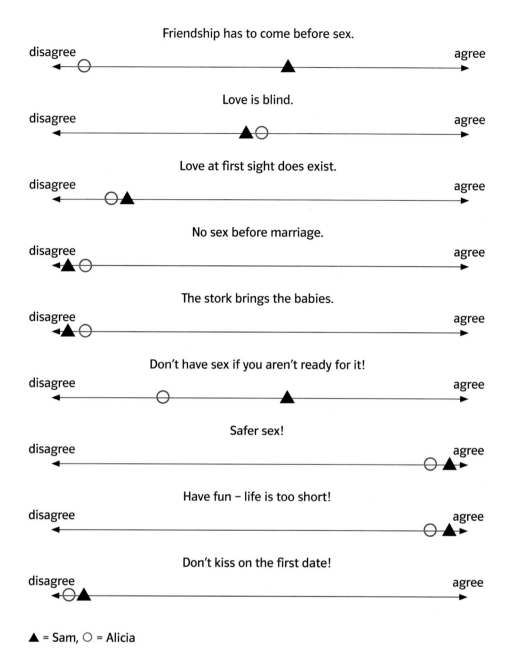

▲ = Sam, ○ = Alicia

II. Modul 2

Methode

Die Auswertung der Ergebnisse der Hausaufgabe kann in der Kugellager Methode erfolgen. Hierzu wird die Klasse in zwei Gruppen geteilt und die Lerngruppe sitzt sich in zwei Stuhlkreisen, einem inneren und einem äußeren, gegenüber. Die Schülerinnen und Schüler einer der beiden Stuhlkreise (z.B. des inneren Kreises) tragen dem jeweils gegenübersitzenden Lernenden die Argumente vor, die dafür sprechen, dass Sam und Alicia sich lieben. Die zuhörenden Schülerinnen und Schüler ergänzen ihre Notizen. Im Anschluss tragen die Partner ihre Argumente vor, die dagegen sprechen. Auf Signal des Lehrers rotieren die beiden Kreise (z.B. alle um zwei Plätze nach rechts). Wieder tragen sich gegenübersitzende Paare ihre Ergebnisse vor. Die SuS, die vorher die Argumente, die dafür sprechen, vorgetragen haben, tragen nun die Argumente vor, die dagegen sprechen. Die SuS, die vorher Argumente, die gegen wirkliche Liebe zwischen Sam und Alicia sprechen, vorgetragen haben, nennen nun die, die dafür sprechen. So wird Eintönigkeit vermieden, der Redeanteil der Schülerinnen und Schüler bei der Besprechung der Hausaufgabe maximiert und gleichzeitig annähernde Vollständigkeit der Ergebnisse gewährleistet.

Fragestellung

Is it really 'love' that Sam and Alicia feel for each other?

Ergebnis

arguments for calling Sam's and Alicia's feelings 'love':
- for both, life means waiting for the next date, everything else loses importance
- they do everything together
- they confess their love to each other
- the only thing Sam wants is to be with Alicia
- he thinks about her all the time
- not seeing each other for one evening is a torture
- Sam is jealous when Alicia does not answer the phone

arguments against calling Sam's and Alicia's feelings 'love':
- Sam just says that he loves Alicia because he does not know what else to say when she confesses her love and finds it rude not to say the same
- adults say that children do not know what love is
- Sam only wants fun, not problems or responsibility which might come along with love

Methode

Die Frage, warum Sams Mutter nicht will, dass Sam und Alicia jede freie Minute miteinander verbringen und die Begründung, die sie Sam gibt, sollte in der Klasse zur Diskussion gestellt werden. Hier können die Schülerinnen und Schüler eigene Meinungen und Erfahrungen einbringen, was zu einer angeregten Diskussion in der Klasse führen dürfte.

Fragestellung

Why does Sam's mother so urgently want an evening with Sam?

II. Modul 2

Ergebnis

"It's not healthy. [...] It gets in the way of things: Friends. Schoolwork. Family.
Skating. ... Everything. Life." (p. 49/50)

Hausaufgaben

a) Read chapters 4 and 5 and collect further arguments for or against calling
   Sam's and Alicia's feelings 'love'.
b) Collect vocabulary from the word field of dating and love and add further
   vocabulary during the course of the novel.

Ergebnis

a) arguments for calling Sam's and Alicia's feelings 'love':
   - Alicia considers Sam part of her family and invites him to lunch when her
     brother comes home from college
   - she keeps sending text messages even though he does not answer

   arguments against calling Sam's and Alicia's feelings 'love':
   - two or three weeks after their first date they get bored with each other
   - they only watch TV and have sex, they hardly ever talk
   - Sam calls it "the same routine" and goes back to his old routines, skating
     and playing Xbox
   - he says he was desperate to sleep with someone but has paid too high a
     price for it
   - he does not want to endure Alicia's parents' condescending talk
   - he says to Mark that their relationship is not really serious

b) Die lesebegleitende Aufgabe kann an jeder Stelle der Unterrichtseinheit
   ausgewertet werden. – Die Sammlung der Vokabeln sollte jedoch nicht in der
   Folgestunde erfolgen, da der lesebegleitende Charakter der Aufgabe erhalten
   bleiben soll. – In der Stunde, in der dann die lesebegleitende Aufgabe b)
   ausgewertet wird, können entweder alle von den Schülerinnen und Schülern
   gefundenen Vokabeln gesammelt werden (z.B. an der Tafel, als *mindmap* oder
   wordweb) oder die Lernenden bestimmen im Schneeballsystem die ihrer
   Meinung nach wichtigsten Vokabeln.

   Beim Schneeballsystem notiert zunächst jeder Schüler die aus seiner/ihrer Sicht
   für den Grundwortschatz 8 wichtigsten Vokabeln. In Partnerarbeit werden
   anschließend aus den jeweils 8 Vokabeln beider Partner die 12 wichtigsten
   bestimmt. Es ist davon auszugehen, dass es Überschneidungen geben wird. Die
   unterschiedlichen Vokabeln müssen von den Schülerinnen und Schülern
   begründet verteidigt werden. In einem dritten Schritt treffen die Paare auf ein
   weiteres Paar und reduzieren die nun insgesamt 24 notierten Vokabeln auf 15.
   Diese werden im Plenum gesammelt (Tafel, Folie, Handout) und dienen als
   Lernwortschatz.

KV 5 dient als Anhaltspunkt für die Lehrkraft, kann aber auch alternativ – falls man
die Sammlung der Vokabeln nicht in der oben beschriebenen Form in Schülerhand
geben will – an die Schülerinnen und Schüler als Lernwortschatz verteilt werden. In
den leeren Zeilen können weitere Wörter ergänzt werden.

Modul 3   Alicia's pregnancy (3-4 Std.)

Lernziel
Sich mit den Konsequenzen einer Teenager-Schwangerschaft auseinandersetzen.

Methode
In den als Hausaufgabe gelesenen Kapiteln 4 und 5 hat Sam gerade erfahren, dass er möglicherweise Vater wird. Statt auf Alicia im Starbucks Cafe zu warten und anschließend den Schwangerschaftstest durchzuführen, schaltet er sein Handy ab, geht nach Hause und feiert mit seinen Eltern seinen sechzehnten Geburtstag. Um den Wortschatz der Schülerinnen und Schüler im Bereich des Ausdrückens von Gefühlen zu erweitern, nehmen die Lernenden einen Perspektivenwechsel vor und sammeln Adjektive, die Alicias Gefühlslage in dieser Situation beschreiben.

Die Sammlung kann zunächst von den Schülerinnen und Schülern in Einzelarbeit, später im Plenum an der Tafel, auf einem Lernplakat oder auf einer Folie erfolgen. Ein Clustern der Wörter wird jedoch schwierig, da die Gefühle alle mehr oder weniger negativ (unglücklich, verwirrt, traurig etc.) sind.

Fragestellung
Alicia's period is three weeks late and she has finally decided to tell Sam and do a pregnancy test. But when returning to the Starbucks' Café Sam is gone. Now, being alone, fearing being pregnant, how does Alicia probably feel?

Ergebnis
- scared, frightened, terrified, afraid
- angry, furious, fuming, outraged
- shocked, surprised
- disappointed
- upset
- worried, concerned
- nervous, uneasy
- sad
- frustrated
- ashamed
- miserable, awkward, wretched, lousy
- unhappy
- lonely, alone
- embarrassed
- bewildered, confused
- sorry
- fed up with Sam/their relationship/life
- responsible/ irresponsible
- hurt
- rejected
- excited
- curious
- regretful
- desperate
- guilty

II. Modul 3

Methode
Nach der Sammlung von Adjektiven, die vermutete Gefühle Alicias beschreiben, überlegen die Schülerinnen und Schüler, welche Möglichkeiten Alicia hätte und welche Entscheidungen sie treffen müsste, wenn sie tatsächlich schwanger wäre. Nach Festhalten der Möglichkeiten an der Tafel, sollen die Lernenden in einem Flussdiagramm darstellen, welche Entscheidungen sie treffen muss. Dazu kann in Kleingruppen von 2-3 Schülerinnen und Schülern gearbeitet werden. Für die Präsentation kann man zu Beginn der Arbeitsphase einem oder mehreren Teams eine Folie zur Verfügung stellen, auf die sie das Flussdiagramm zeichnen. Dieses wird im Anschluss von den Kleingruppen mit Erläuterungen präsentiert. Gegebenenfalls muss man vor der Präsentation *If-clauses Type I* und *II* wiederholen, da diese hier aktiv angewendet werden müssen.

Fragestellung
If she was pregnant, which options would Alicia have?

Ergebnis
a) abortion
b) give the baby up for adoption
c) raise the child as a single mother
d) raise the child as a family (with Sam)
e) …

Aufgabe
Try to visualize the decisions she has to make in a flow chart.

Ergebnis
Das hier dargestellte Flussdiagramm enthält lediglich die vier oben genannten Optionen. Sollten die Schülerinnen und Schüler weitere Vorschläge einbringen, müssen diese dementsprechend in das Diagramm integriert werden.

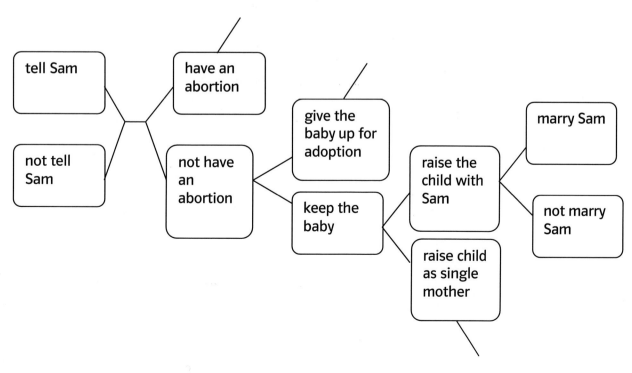

25

II. Modul 3

Methode

Der Leseauftrag, der in der folgenden Hausaufgabe gestellt wird, umfasst etwa 100 Seiten, die Kenntnisse über den Inhalt werden jedoch nicht in der folgenden Stunde benötigt. In leseunerfahrenen Lerngruppen sollte dementsprechend mehr Zeit gegeben werden als von einer zur nächsten Stunde.

Auch der zweite Teil der Hausaufgabe kann an jeder beliebigen Stelle der Unterrichtseinheit besprochen werden. Hier sollen die Schülerinnen und Schüler erneut ihren Wortschatz um das Wortfeld *Sex, pregnancy and birth* erweitern (siehe **KV 6**).

Hausaufgabe

Read chapters 6-9.

Connect verbs and nouns to form meaningful expressions and visualize the connection between these expressions in a flow chart.

Ergebnis

Das hier dargestellte Diagramm kann variieren. Gemeinsam mit den Schülerinnen und Schülern kann eine alternative Lösung an der Tafel entwickelt werden. Wenn man diese Phase verkürzen möchte, kann ein leistungsstärkeres Lerngruppenmitglied das Flussdiagramm bereits zu Hause auf Folie darstellen. Diese kann dann aufgelegt und überprüft sowie ggf. modifiziert werden.

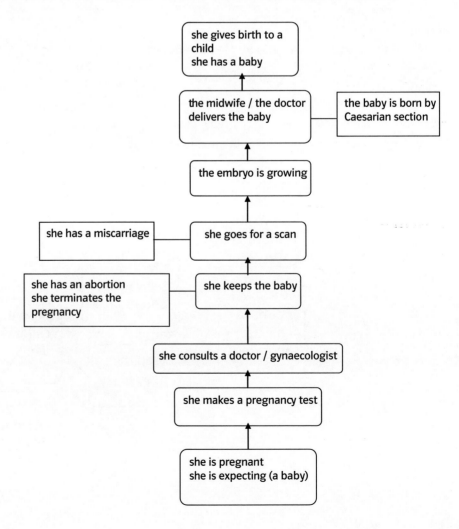

Methode

Nachdem die Schülerinnen und Schüler Alicias Optionen im Falle einer Schwangerschaft zusammengestellt haben, sollen sie nun Argumente für und wider diese Möglichkeiten finden. Aus dem Kontext des Romans heraus ist nicht anzunehmen, dass Alicia die Fragen, die sie an dieser Stelle quälen müssen, mit irgendjemandem bespricht. Da sich bei einem inneren Monolog zur Entscheidungsfindung das Bild von Engelchen und Teufelchen, die links und rechts auf der Schulter sitzen und Argumente liefern, aufdrängt, sollen die Lernenden genau diese beiden Rollen einnehmen.

Dazu werden fünf Gruppen gebildet, die jeweils einen Teil der **KV 7.1** bis **7.5** bearbeiten. Bei entsprechender Größe der Lerngruppe kann man einen Teil der KVs auch an zwei Gruppen vergeben. Die ideale Gruppengröße liegt für diese Aufgabe sicherlich bei 3 Schülern.

Sobald die Kleingruppen die pro und kontra Argumente von Engelchen und Teufelchen zusammengestellt haben, sollen sie sich für ein Rollenspiel vorbereiten, in dem Engelchen und Teufelchen abwechselnd auf Alicia einreden und sie von der jeweiligen Meinung zu überzeugen versuchen. Dieses wird für jede Fragestellung anschließend im Plenum vorgeführt.

Zuletzt sollte die Lerngruppe diskutieren, welche Argumente sie schließlich überzeugt haben und was Alicia im Fall einer Schwangerschaft tatsächlich tun sollte.

Fragestellung

What are the arguments that Alicia has to consider to come to a decision?

Ergebnis

Shall I tell Sam that I am pregnant?

no:
- Perhaps he does not want to see you again.
- He will be a bad father!
- He does not have enough money to raise a baby.
- He could harm the baby.
- Perhaps he would commit suicide or kill you and the baby.
- He is too young/ childish to be a father.
- He will put you under pressure to get an abortion.
- …

yes:
- Sam will call you and he will be very sorry.
- He will have more time for you and he will look after you.
- He will leave school and get a job, so he can pay for all the things the baby needs.
- You will have a partner who you can talk to.
- He will love the baby when it is born.
- He has a right to know that he is going to be a father.
- …

II. Modul 3

Shall I have an abortion?/Shall I give the baby up for adoption?[1]

yes:
- You are young and want to enjoy your life.
- You have to go to school to get an education.
- A child is expensive and you have no money.
- A child means too much responsibility.
- You will have to get up at night and change nappies.
- The baby will cry all the time.
- The baby could spoil your figure.*
- The baby will get on your nerves.
- You won't have any time left for yourself.
- You don't know how to take care of a baby.
- There are a lot of people who won't understand that you had your baby at such a young age.
- Sam will leave you and you will never find a boyfriend again, if you have a baby.
- Children only cause problems.
- You will have your old life back soon.
- You can still have a baby when you are older.
- …

no:
- You kill a human being. *
- You can give the baby up for adoption instead. *
- Your parents, Sam and Sam's mother will help you raise the child.
- You are not alone.
- You can still go out because you have a family who can take care of the baby.
- You can watch your child grow up.
- You had sex without contraception, now you will have to take responsibility for the consequences.
- The baby has a right to live. *
- There are a lot of organizations that can help you if you have problems.
- It is your own flesh and blood.
- It would never be happy in another family. **
- Maybe you can't find a good family for the baby. **
- You will regret it one day when it is too late.
- …

Shall I raise the child on my own?

no:
See arguments in favour of having an abortion/ giving the child up for adoption.

yes:
- Nobody can interfere with your child's upbringing.
- You are still young when your child is a teenager and you can do a lot of things together and make up for your lost years.

---

1 Die Argumente für beide Fragen sind nahezu identisch. Die mit *versehenen Aussagen gelten nur für die Frage „Shall I have an abortion?", die mit ** versehenen Aussagen gelten nur für die Frage „Shall I give the baby up for adoption?".

- Better raise your child alone than with a bad father.
- Only a mother knows what is best for her child.
- There are a lot of organizations that can help you.
- Your parents will be there for you and the baby.
- There are a lot of other single mothers in London. If they can do it, so can you.
- Men will come and go but your child will always love you.
- Sam does not love you anymore.
- ...

Shall I raise the child together with Sam?

no:
- Sam does not really love you.
- Sam will leave as soon as it becomes difficult.
- Sam cannot be a good father.
- Your parents will be a better help than Sam.
- You will have to live with Sam and cook and clean for him.
- What can he do that you can't do on your own?
- ...

yes:
- Your child needs a mother and a father.
- You can share the work between you.
- Sam can get a job and earn some money for you and the baby.
- You can still go to school if Sam looks after the baby.
- He might be a good father.
- If it's a boy, Sam can show him how to skate.
- You need some help to raise a child, you cannot do it alone.
- Sam can also get up if the baby cries at night.
- ...

Aufgabe
Write Alicia's text message to Sam for both cases, pregnant and not pregnant.

Ergebnis
Thanks for being such a great help. You are lucky: I'm not pregnant. And I am glad that I am not having a baby with a wanker like you.
Alicia

or

Just to let you know: I am pregnant! I think we need to talk. Call me!
Alicia

Methode
In der folgenden Aufgabe (siehe **KV 8**) sollen sich die Schülerinnen und Schüler mit den Reaktionen der Eltern und dem, was sie dazu bewegt, auseinandersetzen. Dazu wird zunächst die Textkenntnis überprüft, indem die SuS Zitate der Eltern in ihren Kontext einordnen. Im zweiten Teil der Aufgabe sollen Vermutungen über die Beweggründe der Eltern für ihre Äußerungen angestellt werden. Es sollte deutlich werden, dass die Reaktionen der Eltern auf Alicias Schwangerschaft trotz der

II. Modul 3

unterschiedlichen Familiensituationen (verschiedene Gesellschaftsschichten, verschiedene Bildungsniveaus, unterschiedliches familiäres Umfeld etc.) ähnlich sind.

Diese beiden Aufgabenteile können stichpunktartig in Partnerarbeit bearbeitet werden.

Daran anschließend sollen sich die SuS in einer kreativen Schreibaufgabe der Argumentation und der Stimmungslage der Eltern weiter nähern. Dazu verfasst jeder Schüler einen Text, der den inneren Monolog eines der drei Elternteile wiedergeben soll. Zumindest einige dieser Texte sollten vorgetragen werden, wobei die Mitschüler beurteilen sollten, wie authentisch jeder Text im Hinblick auf die jeweilige Romanfigur erscheint.

Abschließend sollten die Schülerinnen und Schüler sich dazu äußern, wie vernünftig die Eltern sich ihrer Meinung nach in dieser Situation verhalten.

Fragestellung
Is the parents' reaction to the news reasonable or unreasonable?

Ergebnis
a) und b)

- "Thirty-two. So she was sixteen when you were born. ... Jesus Christ. Don't you people ever learn anything?"
  ⇨ Alicia's father to Sam (p. 141).

  He has just found out that Sam's mother was a teenager, too, when she gave birth to Sam. He tries to humiliate Sam by calling him and his mother "you people", which implies that they are from a lower class than Alicia's family and that all children from teenage parents will be teenage parents again because they are no good and do not learn from their mistakes.

- "Do you hate us? Is that what this is about?"
  ⇨ Alicia's mother to Sam (p. 139).

  Alicia's mother insinuates that Sam has deliberately made Alicia pregnant because this was the only way to keep her as a girlfriend. She, like her husband, implies that their family is something better than Sam's so he would be unable to find a girlfriend like Alicia ever again. She also implies that Sam has made her pregnant out of sheer hate for the upper-middle class, worrying that a teenage pregnancy will not only destroy Alicia's future but, above all, her parents' reputation.

- "How did this happen? I presumed you were having sex. I didn't think you were too stupid to use contraception."
  ⇨ Alicia's mother to Sam and Alicia (p. 140).

  After Alicia has told her parents that it was Sam who did not want to be with her, not the other way round, her mother cannot believe that it might have been Alicia who became pregnant deliberately just because she wanted to keep Sam.

30

- "Of all the things you could do. All the ways you could hurt me."
  ⇨ Sam's mother to Sam (p. 144).

After Sam's mother has started crying about the news of Alicia's pregnancy, she finally starts talking. She still thinks that Sam ran away because of his unhappy childhood. So she presumes that after all the talking about how hard it was for her to raise a baby as a teenage mother, he must have deliberately made Alicia pregnant to hurt her.

- "Here's a good way of not getting someone pregnant: Don't have sex with them."
  ⇨ Sam's mother to Sam (p.144).

This is his mother's pragmatic and sarcastic answer to Sam's affirmation that he did not get Alicia pregnant just to hurt her. It is advice nobody can argue with.

c) Alicia's father/mother:

That girl is so stupid! I knew from the beginning that this boy is not good for her. I/She shouldn't have invited these people to my/her birthday party. I mean, why associate with them anyway. Those people are so below us. I should have known that they would get us into trouble sooner or later.

Alicia could have gone to university. She could have done a degree like us, like her brother, and she would have had a future. Going out with this skateboard guy was a bad idea from the beginning. Why did we allow that in the first place? She is still too young to make decisions like this on her own.

We should have known that they are having sex. All this hanging around in Alicia's room … God knows how many other girls he might have made pregnant. We should have given her a better sex education. I thought they learn about contraception and stuff like that at school!

And what a stupid idea to keep the baby! They are too young to be parents! Where will they live? And how is he going to pay for it all? I never thought I would be a grandparent under these circumstances …

Sam's mother:

I knew it. That girl was not good for Sam! She looks pretty, right, and I can see how he fell for her, but she is a little daft, too. I shouldn't have taken him to that party. It's all my own fault.

But after all that talking about how hard it was for me to raise him all alone… How could he be so reckless about contraception? Didn't he learn anything from my mistakes? Now that we are finally over the worst and my life is starting to look up again … What will Mark say that he is dating a grandmother? Oh my God, I am going to be a grandmother at 32. I am four years younger than Jennifer Aniston and the same age as Cameron Diaz and I am going to be a grandmother …

He just did that to hurt me because I screwed up his life, too. But didn't I do my best raising a child on my own with a father who was useless? It's all his father's fault. If he had been a better father, all this wouldn't have happened! My son was supposed to have a better future than I had and he threw it all away …

II.   Modul 4

Modul 4   Learning to cope with the pregnancy (1 Std.)

Lernziel
Die Inhalte der Kapitel 10 bis 12 wiedergeben können und den Zweck der
Zukunftsvisionen Sams erkennen.

Methode
Kapitel 10 bis 12 handeln von den Wochen nachdem Sam und Alicia ihren Eltern
von der Schwangerschaft erzählt haben. Außer einem neuen Transport in die
Zukunft passiert nichts Wesentliches, aber die Beziehung von Sam und Alicia
entwickelt sich weiter, was zum Schluss dieser Unterrichtseinheit von den
Schülerinnen und Schülern benannt und bewertet werden soll. Zunächst wird in
diesen Kapiteln das Leseverständnis der Schülerinnen und Schüler überprüft. Dies
kann anhand von **KV 9** lesebegleitend geschehen, das heißt die Lernenden füllen
KV 9 als Hausaufgabe während des Lesens aus, oder das Arbeitsblatt wird zur
Besprechung des Gelesenen in der Folgestunde eingesetzt. Die Aufgaben zu den
Kapiteln 11 und 12 sowie die Anschlussfragen können ggf. auch mündlich statt
schriftlich bearbeitet werden.

Bei der Besprechung der Anschlussfragen sollte über den Zweck der Zeitreisen
hinaus auch eine Bewertung dieses literarischen Mittels erfolgen. Des weiteren
sollte den Schülerinnen und Schülern Raum zur Äußerung ihrer Gedanken im
Zusammenhang mit den Zeitreisen gegeben werden.

Fragestellung
How does Sam's and Alicia's relationship develop in the next few weeks?

Hausaufgabe
Read chapters 10 to 12 and do the tasks on worksheet 9.

Ergebnis
Chapter 10 (correct order):
* His mum tells his father about the pregnancy. He takes it easy and with humour. (3)
* They find out about it at school and surprisingly even the teachers are inter-
  ested as they want to try out a new programme for teenage parents. (6)
* Sam and Alicia go to a scan and find out the baby is a boy. (5)
* They kiss on the way home and decide to get back together, but don't have a
  sexual relationship anymore. (2)
* They go to a maternity class and feel out of place because the other parents-to-
  be are much older. (1)
* Mark moves in with Sam and his mother. (4)

Chapter 11:
Alicia's parents think that Sam <u>destroyed</u> their daughter's life, <u>but</u> they make an
effort to be nice, which means they keep on talking about <u>the future</u>. They <u>try to
treat</u> Sam <u>as a</u> part of their family now, <u>but</u> they are <u>surprised</u> that Sam and Alicia
want to live together in <u>their</u> house when the baby is born and accept this. That
night, Sam goes <u>skating</u> for the first time in a while. His friend <u>Rubbish</u> tells him
that he thinks Sam screwed up his life <u>and</u> Sam realizes how <u>perfect</u> his life was

32

before. When he comes home, Sam's mother tries to talk him out of <u>moving in with</u> Alicia but after asking <u>TH</u> for advice, he shows responsibility.

Chapter 12:
Sam is whizzed into the <u>future</u> again:

He doesn't live with Alicia anymore and he has a little <u>baby sister</u>. One morning he gets a <u>phone call</u> from Alicia. She is ill, so Sam has to take Roof to the doctor's to get a <u>jab</u>. Sam messes up because he does not know <u>his son's proper name</u>. He spends the afternoon with his son going to the playground, where he finds out why Roof does not like the <u>swings</u> there. He buys him a useless helicopter at a <u>toyshop</u> and watches a movie called <u>Dressing Salad</u> with him, which they have to leave after a few minutes because Roof does not like it. In the evening, Sam realizes he is looking forward to meeting his son in reality. His mother confirms that Sam is doing alright and has not messed up his life completely. She gives him a mark of <u>seven</u> out of ten.

Question 1:
The author's reason for introducing this kind of time travel might be to
- find a means to contrast Sam's present life with his future life more strongly,
- show Sam that he has not messed up his life completely,
- erase his doubts,
- encourage him,
- show him what he needs to learn in order not to fail,
- …

Question 2:
More than seven out of ten because
- he goes to college and does not neglect his education.
- he tries to be a good father.
- he plays with Roof and takes him to the doctor. It is not his fault that he fails.
- he does not quit his hobby.
- he is a loving brother.
- …

Less than seven out of ten because
- he does not live with Alicia anymore, so he leaves her alone with most of the work.
- he does not even know his son's proper name.
- he caused the accident Roof had with the swings.
- he does not go to college regularly.
- he goes skating instead of helping Alicia with the baby.
- he does not know that a nearly two year-old is too young for the cinema.
- he wastes the little money he has on stupid toys just to calm Roof.
- …

→ How does Sam's and Alicia's relationship develop in the next few weeks?
- They get together again and try to cope with the new and difficult situation.
- They seem to have matured and seem to be on the way to a good "working relationship".
- …

II. Modul 5

Lernziel

Den Rest des Romans mit verschiedenen Leseaufträgen selbstständig lesen.

Methode

Da die Schülerinnen und Schüler sich nun eingelesen haben und im weiteren Verlauf des Romans keine neuen Themen mehr auftauchen bzw. keine dringend zu besprechenden Ereignisse mehr passieren, muss der Rest der Lektüre nicht mehr schrittweise von der Lehrkraft/im Unterricht begleitet werden. Um ein detailliertes Textverständnis sicherzustellen, sollten jedoch Verständnisaufgaben gestellt werden. Zu den Kapiteln 10 bis 12 haben die Schülerinnen und Schüler bereits verschiedene Formen von *comprehension tasks* kennengelernt, **KV 10** liefert weitere Vorschläge. Die letzten acht Kapitel (13-20) werden nun im Sinne vom ‚Lernen durch Lehren' unter den Lernenden aufgeteilt, die jeweils eine der Aufgabenstellungen von **KV 10** auswählen, und vorbereiten (je nach Klassenstärke in Kleingruppen oder an einzelne Schülerinnen und Schüler). Im Anschluss an das folgende Modul (siehe *Wrapping up the novel*) wird so dass Textverständnis der Mitschüler/innen überprüft.

Hausaufgabe

Finish reading the novel within the next two weeks and prepare a comprehension task for the class for the chapter you've been given.

Modul 5   Preventing teenage pregnancy (4-5 Std.)

Lernziel

Das Ausmaß der Problematik in UK erkennen, Medienkampagnen kennenlernen und bewerten.

Methode

In Kapitel 10 erwähnt Sam, dass die Lehrer seiner Schule überraschenderweise Interesse an der Schwangerschaft seiner Freundin zeigen, da es ein neues Regierungsprogramm zum Thema *teenage pregnancy* gibt, das sie ausprobieren möchten (siehe S. 150). Die Strategien dieses Programms werden auf **KV 11** vorgestellt.

Da die Zahlen (46,6 Schwangerschaften pro 1000 15-17-jährigen Mädchen) für Schülerinnen und Schüler meist etwas abstrakt sind, sollte die Lehrperson an dieser Stelle die Bedeutung dieser Information noch einmal verdeutlichen:

1998 war etwa jedes 21. Mädchen zwischen 15 und 17 in Großbritannien schwanger. Als Zahlenspiel kann man nun überlegen, wie viele Schwangerschaften dies in der Lerngruppe, in der Jahrgangsstufe oder an der Schule ungefähr wären.

Anschließend sollen die Schülerinnen und Schüler die fünf Elemente des Programms charakterisieren und evaluieren. Hierzu bietet sich die *Think-Pair-Share* Methode an, da auf diese Art und Weise alle Lernenden ins Unterrichtsgeschehen integriert sind. In der *Think*-Phase bearbeitet zunächst jedes Lerngruppenmitglied die Aufgabenstellung in Einzelarbeit. Es ist sinnvoll, die Schülerinnen und Schüler Notizen zu ihren Überlegungen machen zu lassen. In der *Pair*-Phase tauschen die Lernenden ihre Ergebnisse mit einem Partner aus und ergänzen ihre Notizen. In

II.   Modul 5

der *Share*-Phase werden die Ergebnisse im Plenum besprochen. Da sich jeder bereits mit einem Partner ausgetauscht hat, sind die Hemmungen, in der Fremdsprache zu reden oder inhaltliche Fehler zu machen, geringer, so dass sich jeder Lernende beteiligen kann.

Fragestellung

What could strategies to reduce teenage pregnancy in the UK look like?

Ergebnis

	strategy might include	chances of helping to reduce teenage pregnancy (+++ = very good; --- = very small)
Joint action	schools work together with other organizations such as the government's health department, media, producers of contraceptives etc.	+++ the more organizations join in, the more effective the campaign will become
National Media Campaign	TV and print advertisements promoting the use of contraceptives and helplines for teenagers who have questions about contraception	+++ drawing attention to the problem might help to reduce it
Support for the parents of teenagers	helplines to help parents with the sex education of their children	– if parents are ignorant about the sex education of their children, they won't call the helpline anyway
Prevention (including improving sex and relationship education and access to contraception)	a national school curriculum for sex and relationship education, access to contraception at places with lots of teenagers (schools, youth clubs etc.)	+++ the more knowledge a teenager has about pregnancies and sexually transmitted diseases, the less irresponsible they might behave; if they have easy access to contraception, they might use it
Support for teenage parents	helplines, childcare courses, maternity courses, organization of playgroups to enable the teenage parents to get an education, housing opportunities if the teenage parents have to leave their homes etc.	--- too late to prevent pregnancy

Methode

Im Rahmen des Regierungsprogramms zur Reduzierung von Teenager-Schwangerschaften gibt es diverse regierungsgestützte Medienkampagnen in Großbritannien mit unterschiedlichen Adressaten. Da die Recherche mehrerer Kampagnen sehr zeitaufwändig ist, es sich aber aufgrund der unterschiedlichen Zielgruppen durchaus lohnt, mehrere Initiativen zu untersuchen, sollte dies arbeitsteilig geschehen. Auch die Untersuchung einer amerikanischen Kampagne, die den Verzicht auf Sex vor der Ehe propagiert, bietet sich zum Vergleich mit den britischen Initiativen an (siehe **KV 13**).

II. Modul 5

Die Gruppengröße richtet sich nach der Größe der Lerngruppe, mehr als 4-5 Lernende pro Gruppe sind jedoch nicht arbeitsförderlich. Daher müssen ggf. Themen doppelt vergeben werden. Die Art und Weise der Präsentation kann wahlweise von der Lehrkraft vorgegeben werden (z.B. internetgestützt, so dass man Elemente der Kampagne zeigen und kommentieren kann; als Rollenspiel, in dem Jugendliche sich über die Kampagne unterhalten; mit einem Plakat, das die wichtigsten Erkenntnisse präsentiert etc.) oder den Schülerinnen und Schülern frei überlassen werden. Oft gibt es auf diese Weise kreative und überraschende Ergebnisse.

Zur gemeinsamen Evaluation der Präsentationen kann **KV 14** benutzt werden.

Ein kurzer Überblick über die zu recherchierenden Kampagnen:

Die ‚RU Thinking'-Kampagne richtet sich an jüngere Teenager und vertritt die Devise, den ersten Geschlechtsverkehr so lange wie möglich aufzuschieben und dem Druck durch Gleichaltrige standzuhalten. Die Homepage ist unterteilt in *Lad Pad* („Jungs-Bude") und *Lady Lounge*, sowie dort jeweils in die Bereiche *Thinking about your first time?* und *Want to know more about sex?*. Hier werden in altersgemäßer Weise alle Fragen zum Thema Pubertät, Beziehungen, Verhütung, Sex, Ängste und Sehnsüchte, Geschlechtskrankheiten etc. beantwortet. Es gibt außerdem eine Liste von *Essentials*, also der meist gesuchten Stichwörter auf dieser Seite, sowie verschiedene Notfallpläne, die man befolgen sollte, wenn man z.B. glaubt eine Geschlechtskrankheit zu haben, schwanger zu sein usw.

Die *Want Respect? Use a Condom*-Kampagne richtet sich an bereits sexuell aktive Jugendliche und propagiert, wie der Titel bereits deutlich macht, den Gebrauch von Kondomen. In zwei Fernsehspots sieht man einen Jungen, der mit seinen Freunden auf dem Weg zum Fußballplatz ist und sich über seine letzte Nacht mit einem Mädchen unterhält, sowie das Mädchen und eine Freundin, die die selbe Nacht Revue passieren lassen. In einem Spot hat das Pärchen ein Kondom benutzt. Das Mädchen ist glücklich, der Junge erntet Anerkennung bei seinen Freunden. In dem anderen Spot haben die beiden kein Kondom benutzt. Das Mädchen ist unglücklich, hat Angst vor einer Schwangerschaft, der Junge erntet Verachtung bei seinen Freunden. Außerdem wurden im Rahmen der Kampagne Jugendliche zu *peer communicators* im Bereich Sexualerziehung ausgebildet.

Die *Time to Talk*-Kampagne richtet sich an Eltern und bietet Unterstützung für die Erziehung ihrer Kinder im Allgemeinen, jedoch auch im Bereich Sex und Beziehungen. Dabei bietet die Homepage seitenweise Tipps, interaktive Rollenspiele, Comics mit typischen Gesprächssituationen, aber auch Email-Kontakt und Telefon Hotlines sowie Selbsthilfegruppen.

Die amerikanische Kampagne *Teen Choices* bietet ähnlich wie *RU Thinking* ein umfassendes Angebot an Informationen über Sex, Beziehungen, Geschlechtskrankheiten, Verhütung, psychologische Fragen usw. Allerdings legt die Kampagne einen deutlichen Schwerpunkt auf die Verbreitung des kein-Sex-vor-der-Ehe-Gedankens. So wird z.B. bei der Interpretation von Statistiken anders als in Großbritannien hervorgehoben, wie viel Prozent der amerikanischen Jugendlichen noch nie Geschlechtsverkehr hatten, wie viel Prozent ihrer Meinung nach zu früh Geschlechtsverkehr hatten, in wie vielen Staaten Sex vor der Volljährigkeit illegal ist etc. (siehe *Facts about sexually active teens*). Dieser Unterschied sollte bei der

Besprechung der Kampagnen deutlich herausgearbeitet werden. Da die Gruppe jedoch bei der Recherche aufgrund ihrer Unkenntnis der britischen Kampagnen dies nicht vermag, muss die Lehrkraft anschließend das Gespräch initiieren (siehe Fragestellung oben). Des Weiteren schauen die Schülerinnen und Schüler einen (Fernseh?-/Internet?-) *Spot Just say no to sex*, in dem College Studenten und Studentinnen sich zu sexueller Abstinenz bekennen.

Jedoch ist an dieser Stelle zu erwähnen, dass es weitere, neutralere U.S. Kampagnen gibt, z.B. *The National Campaign to Prevent Teen and Unplanned Pregnancy*: http://www.thenationalcampaign.org. Diese arbeitet u.a. mit *MTV* zusammen, die ab Sommer 2009 eine neue Doku-Serie, *16 and pregnant*, über die Herausforderungen einer Teenager Schwangerschaft senden. Zum Zeitpunkt der Erstellung dieses *Teacher's Guides* waren die Folgen noch nicht gesendet, ein Blick ins Internet (www.mtv.com oder www.youtube.com) lohnt sich jedoch sicherlich, da *MTV* aus der Welt der Jugendlichen nicht mehr wegzudenken ist.

Auch den Werbetrailer für die Sendung, den MTV in eine nicht ganz ernstzunehmende Werbung für eine *studying cradle* verpackt hat (was allerdings nicht auf den ersten Blick erkennbar ist und damit zunächst entsetztes Staunen hervorruft), kann als Kontrast zu den christlicheren U.S. Kampagnen eingesetzt werden.

http://16pregnant.mtv.de/videos/16-pregnant-kauftipp-1/4881-lang-version

Fragestellungen
What are the differences between the British and the American campaigns?
Can you find an explanation for these differences?

Ergebnis
- the American campaigns clearly focus on abstinence rather than on contraception as in the British campaigns
- the American message of "no sex before marriage" is clearly visible in their campaigns
- possible explanations: – conservative and religious background of parts of the American population – a radical approach might seem more promising than just giving information
- background: The USA have the highest rate of teenage pregnancies in the entire western world. 3 out of 10 girls become pregnant at least once before their 20th birthday.

Methode
Um festzustellen, wie erfolgreich die Kampagne der britischen Regierung tatsächlich war, analysieren die Schülerinnen und Schüler mithilfe von **KV 12** das statistische Material im Anhang der Textausgabe in Partnerarbeit. Dazu machen sie Notizen, damit die Ergebnisse mit dem passenden Fachvokabular anschließend im Plenum besprochen werden können. Die Frage, ob die Regierungskampagne erfolgreich war, kann mündlich oder schriftlich beantwortet werden. Es sollte dabei auch darauf geachtet werden, dass die SuS positive oder negative statistische Werte nicht ausschließlich mit den Kampagnen in kausalen Zusammenhang bringen.

II. Modul 5

Es bietet sich bei den Statistiken an, die Größenordnungen auf die Schülerzahlen des Jahrgangs oder der Oberstufe zu übertragen. Nimmt man an, eine Schule hat in den Jahrgangsstufen 9 bis 13 250 Schülerinnen (Jahrgangsstärke von 100, 50% davon Mädchen), dann gäbe es darunter jedes Jahr 15-16 Schwangerschaften. Wie viele davon ausgetragen werden, zeigt die letzte Statistik.

Aufgabe

Analyse the tables, graphs and charts about teenage pregnancy in the appendix of the novel (pp. 259-261).

Discuss how successful the government's campaign to reduce teenage pregnancy was and try to find reasons for this.

Fragestellung

Can the British campaigns be considered successful?

Ergebnis

Conception by age of woman at conception
- line graph
- little development in the numbers for under 18s and under 16s
- under 20s: since 2001 steady increase in conceptions per year
- conclusion: the campaigns have not worked, annually even more young women between 18 and 20 have become pregnant since the start of the campaign

Conception rates by age of woman at conception
- table
- a slight downward trend in the conception rates within the age-group of the under 16s, reaching its low point in 2004, since then increase to the same rates as in 2000
- gradual decrease in the conception rates of the under 18s from 2000 to 2006, then rise to 41,9 in 1000
- rise from 2006 to 2007 in the age-group of the under 16s
- falling rates in the conception rates within the age group of the under 20s except for an increase from 2006 to 2007
- altogether every 16th British woman below the age of 20 became pregnant in 2007, every 25th woman below the age of 18 and every 125th woman below the age of 16
- conclusion: initially the campaigns may have had a small effect, but rising rates could indicate that teenagers have become apathetic towards the campaigns

Percentage terminated by abortion
- bar chart
- compared to 2000, about 7% more abortions in the age-group of the under 16s
  => more than 6 in 10 pregnancies in that age group are terminated
- increase of about 5% in the age-group of the under 18s
  => every second pregnancy in that age group was terminated
- increase of about 3% in the age-group of the under 20s
  => more than 4 in 10 pregnancies in that age group are terminated
- conclusion: possible effect of the campaigns: more abortions rather than fewer teenage pregnancies

- teenagers may have gathered from the campaigns that it is hard to be teenage parents
- they still do little to prevent a conception but put up with a termination of the pregnancy instead

Possible reasons for failure of campaigns:
- campaigns do not appeal to teenagers
- too much campaigning could be counter-productive as teenagers want to revolt and ignore adults' advice and appeals
- campaigning is not sufficiently noticed by the teenagers
- easy termination of pregnancy might encourage lack of interest in contraception
- peer pressure to have sex at an early age is higher than the appeal of the campaigns

Methode

Um die Ergebnisse der bisherigen Untersuchungen der Kampagnen in Zusammenhang zu bringen, bietet eine Talk Show zum Thema *Preventing teenage pregnancy* eine Alternative zur im Fremdsprachenunterricht immer wiederkehrenden Frage *What do you think?*

Es werden zunächst vier Experten (jeweils einer, der für eine der vorgestellten Kampagnen spricht) und ein Moderator bestimmt. Die restliche Lerngruppe stellt das Publikum dar, das jedoch nicht stumm zuhört, sondern Fragen an die Experten vorbereitet und sich so und mit ihrer eigenen Meinung an der Diskussion beteiligt.

Nachdem der Moderator die Show eröffnet und die Experten vorgestellt hat, darf zunächst jeder Experte ein kurzes Statement abgeben, wie seine Kampagne die Reduzierung von Teenager Schwangerschaften unterstützt. Dann wird die Diskussion eröffnet, an der sich das Publikum rege beteiligen soll. Zum Schluss fasst der Moderator noch einmal die Argumente zusammen und das Publikum stimmt ab, welche Kampagne die vielversprechendste ist.

Eine Anleitung zur Vorgehensweise sowie sprachliche Mittel befindet sich in **KV 15** und **KV 16**.

Fragestellungen

How do the campaigns appeal to you as teenagers?
What kind of campaign do you think would be most effective?

Alternative

Alternativ kann an dieser Stelle auch die (zum Zeitpunkt der Erstellung dieses Lehrerhandbuchs) neueste Kampagne der britischen Regierung angeschaut und evaluiert werden. Es handelt sich dabei um ein You Tube-Video, das den Anschein macht, als wäre es mit einer Handykamera auf dem Schulhof gedreht worden. Eine Horde Schülerinnen und Schüler stürmen zu einer Menschentraube, die auf den ersten Blick nach den Zuschauern einer Schulhofrauferei aussieht. Es stellt sich jedoch heraus, dass sich die Schülerinnen und Schüler um eine Mitschülerin versammelt haben, die gerade auf dem Schulhof ein Baby zur Welt bringt.

II.　Modul 6

Die Kampagne mit ihren eindeutigen und schockierenden Bildern hat unterschiedliche Reaktionen in Großbritannien hervorgerufen, die in einer kanadischen Nachrichtensendung verarbeitet werden. Unter dem folgenden Link findet man sowohl einen Zeitungsartikel aus dem Ottawa Citizen als auch einen Video Stream der Nachrichtensendung und des You Tube-Videos:

http://www.ottawacitizen.com/Health/Teen+pregnancy+target+YouTube+plo y/1621625/story.html

Das Video kann zum Vergleich mit den anderen Kampagnen gezeigt und dessen Effektivität beurteilt werden; der Zeitungsartikel kann als Hausaufgabe zusammengefasst oder die Nachrichtensendung kommentiert werden.

Modul 6　Wrapping up the novel (3 Std.)

Lernziel
Wichtige Kernpunkte am Ende der Lektüre erkennen und auswerten.

Methode
Nachdem die Schülerinnen und Schüler ihre Leseverständnisüberprüfungen anhand der einige Stunden vorher verteilten Hausaufgabe auf **KV 10** durchgeführt haben und eventuelle Missverständnisse geklärt werden konnten, werden im Unterrichtsgespräch weitere Fragen zum Gesamtwerk (Struktur, Charaktere, Plot etc.) besprochen.

Alternativ können auch die Aufgaben 2 bis 7 als Stummes Schreibgespräch bearbeitet werden. Dazu schreibt die Lehrkraft jeweils eine der Aufgaben auf einen DIN A2-Bogen Papier. Diese werden auf verschiedenen Tischen im Klassenraum ausgelegt. Die Schülerinnen und Schüler verteilen sich gleichmäßig an den Tischen und bearbeiten stumm die Aufgabe. Sobald sie fertig sind, gehen sie zu einem weiteren Tisch und lösen die Aufgabe bzw. schreiben eine Reaktion auf eine bereits notierte Antwort. Die Schülerinnen und Schüler rotieren so lange, bis jeder mindestens einmal an jedem Tisch eine Lösung geschrieben hat. Auf diese Weise können Meinungen kreativ ausgetauscht werden und jeder Schüler ist in diesen Prozess involviert. Am Ende sollten die Lernenden die Möglichkeit bekommen, im Galeriegang alle Ergebnisse noch einmal zu sichten und evtl. Reaktionen auf eigene Antworten zu lesen.

Auf der Basis der so gesicherten Textkenntnis sollten nun im Unterrichtsgespräch Fragen besprochen werden, die nach Meinung der SuS noch offen sind oder auch vom Roman bis zu seinem Ende offen gelassen werden. Wichtig ist, dass die SuS in dieser Phase der Besprechung selbst mit Fragen an den Text und die Lerngruppe herantreten.

Für den Fall, dass es den SuS schwerfällt, selbstständig eine Fragehaltung zu entwickeln, sind im Anschluss einige Fragen aufgeführt, mit denen eine Diskussion und weitere Fragen angestoßen werden könnten.

Fragestellung

Sam says, "… telling a story is more difficult than it looks, because you don't know what to put where." What has the author put where? What might have been his intention in doing so?

Ergebnis

Structure of the novel

1	Introduction
2-5	Development of Sam's and Alicia's relationship
6	1st whizz into the future: One of the first nights with the baby.
7-8	Sam runs away
9-11	Coping with the pregnancy
12	2nd whizz into the future: Spending an afternoon with the toddler
13-18	Birth/Learning to be a parent
19	Some time later: Update on events
20	3rd whizz into the future: Sam, Alicia and their new partners meet

Possible intentions:

- Whizzes into the future for the reader to keep up the tension.
  - Will it really happen?
  - How will Sam cope with the situation?
  - Funny effect of Sam not knowing what to do/say.
  - Keep an open ending.
  - Positive outlook into their future etc.
- Point of view: some time later
  - Not being in the middle of events and looking back instead might make the narrator seem more objective than he would be in a certain situation.

Fragestellung

Would you like to have Sam's ability to see into the future?

Ergebnis

– Yes, because it gives you the possibility to plan your life, you might be motivated to work hard, probably to change your life for the better, to avoid mistakes etc.

– No, because there won't be any surprises, which makes your life boring; you might be too paralyzed to act or to change anything.

Fragestellung

In chapter 3 (p. 49), Sam says, "I can't be bad." Is he being honest with himself? Does he change over the course of the novel?

II. Modul 6

Ergebnis

- situation: his mother wants him to spend an evening with her (and not with Alicia)
- he tries to find an excuse but cannot because he does not want to make his mother feel bad
- his explanation: being bad is something you do on purpose => honest with himself, as he doesn't act with bad intentions
- makes 'mistakes' like running away
- his reactions are plausible, but not mature
- in the end, he stands up for the things he did wrong and copes with his life quite well
- Note: In an interview with *The Atlantic* from November 2007 (see Appendix of the novel, p. 262 f.) Hornby says that a protagonist's willingness to redemption is very important to him.

Fragestellungen

What's Sam's experience with his parents?

How does it influence his own role as a father?

Ergebnis

- Sam's mother became pregnant at the age of 16.
- His parents married, got divorced and Sam's father was never there for him afterwards.
  => "I was born with just a mum." (p. 224)
- his mum has always been a good mother to him and he knows that her life as a single mother was not easy
- parents are role models or the complete opposite for their children
  => Sam wants to copy the kind of parent his mother was for him and be the opposite of his father
- because of his parents' experience he does not want to marry Alicia or stay with her at all costs
- his guilty conscience about not telling Alicia that "it half happened" also influences his efforts to be a good father for Roof

Fragestellung

Did Alicia make the right decision in keeping her baby?

Ergebnis

- under the circumstances, Sam and Alicia cope quite well as teenage parents:
  - both go to college
  - they have found new partners who seem to like their son
  - they get on well with each other
  - they manage to take care of Roof with the help of their parents
- however, both their lives would have been easier without a child

Fragestellung

Will Sam still be in touch with Roof fifteen years later?

Ergebnis

Most likely he will.

- he decides not to be one of the 80% of teenage fathers who lose touch with their child (see p. 233)
- possible difficulties: geographical distance after moving, new partners
- knowing about these difficulties will help Sam keep in contact with Roof

Fragestellung

Why did Hornby choose the word "slam" as the title of his book? What does he refer to?

Ergebnis

The word "slam" has several meanings:

- to move against a hard surface with force and usually a loud noise, also referring to falling while skateboarding
- to criticize harshly; a cutting and violent criticism
- a sudden loud noise

- Sam uses the word while talking to his friend Rabbit who is skating at Grind City (see p. 38)
- the word could also refer to the sexual intercourse that leads to Alicia's pregnancy
- even though Sam keeps quiet about what "half happened", their lives as teenagers end with a slam
- => the title links skateboarding and the unwanted teenage pregnancy

Anmerkung: Dass und warum der Autor gegenüber seinen Charakteren und seinen Lesern keinen moralischen Zeigefinger erheben möchte, legt er in einem Interview dar, das er im November 2007 gab (siehe S. 262 ff. der Textausgabe).

Methode

Nach dem Bearbeiten einer Unterrichtslektüre möchten die Schülerinnen und Schüler im Allgemeinen gern ihre Meinung zum Buch kundtun. Für die Lehrkraft ist dies möglicherweise eine wichtige Information für die Auswahl der nächsten Lektüre. Im Unterrichtsgespräch bekommt man häufig keine sehr differenzierte Stellungnahme von Seiten der Lernenden, daher empfiehlt sich an dieser Stelle eine Buchbesprechung, evtl. mit anschließender Präsentation oder nur für die Hand der Lehrkraft. Eine Anleitung zur Vorgehensweise befindet sich auf **KV 17**. Buchbesprechungen findet man zu Hauf im Internet.

Aufgabe

Write a book review about the novel.

II.   Modul 7

Post-reading activities (6-15 Stunden)

Modul 7   "Juno" (5-6 Std.)

Der 2008 erschienene Film „Juno" erzählt die Geschichte einer selbstbewussten sechzehnjährigen Schülerin, die beim ersten Sex mit ihrem verklemmten und ‚Tictac'-süchtigen Freund schwanger wird. Da eine Abtreibung für sie ebenso wenig in Frage kommt, wie das Aufziehen des Kindes, entscheidet sich Juno, das Kind zur Adoption freizugeben. Junos Anwesenheit im Leben der zukünftigen Adoptiveltern, einem reichen kinderlosen Paar aus der Vorstadt, sorgt jedoch für reichlich Turbulenzen (siehe auch deutsche Filmbesprechung **KV 20**).

Der Einsatz des Films eignet sich an dieser Stelle nicht nur zur Abrundung der Unterrichtseinheit im Allgemeinen, sondern bietet vor allem zahlreiche Vergleichsmöglichkeiten mit der Lektüre. Die Schwangerschaft wird im Wesentlichen aus der Perspektive des schwangeren Mädchens dargestellt – über den Vater und dessen Gefühle erfahren wir, ebenso wie in *Slam* über Alicia, nur recht wenig – der Zuschauer erfährt aber außerdem von den Schwierigkeiten, die eine Adoption anstelle des Aufziehens des Kindes mit sich bringen kann.

Lernziel
Eine Teenager-Schwangerschaft aus der Sicht der jungen Mutter kennenlernen und mit der Sicht des jungen Vaters in *Slam* vergleichen.

Methode
Zur Einstimmung auf den Film zeigt die Lehrkraft eine Kopie von **KV 18**. Die Schülerinnen und Schüler beschreiben und vergleichen beide Filmplakate, entscheiden, welches der beiden Plakate sie mehr anspricht und äußern begründete Vermutungen, worum es in dem Film geht.

Fragestellungen
Which of the two posters do you find more appealing?
What do you expect the film to be about?

Ergebnis
The English poster:
- teenage girl, about 15 or 16 years old
- obviously pregnant and with typical posture of a pregnant woman
- baggy jeans, skirt worn over her jeans, t-shirt, dark hooded jacket
- ponytail, facial expression: cool, almost conceited
- teenage boy, also about 15 or 16 years old
- clothes: sports outfit with shorts, sweat bands round his head and wrists, t-shirt, sports socks, trainers
- he is scratching, looking insecure and confused
- background stripes, just like the girl's t-shirt or the American flag
- on the top: actors starring in the movie, at the bottom: credits and the release month of the film
- title: middle right of the poster
- subheading
- reference to the director's earlier movie

44

II. Modul 7

- testimonial from well-known film critic
- at the bottom right: tiny silhouettes of eight people running

The German poster:
- girl and boy have moved to the centre of the poster, only the upper halves of their bodies can be seen
- behind them: a younger couple on the left, an older couple on the right; the young woman and the older man are smiling, the young man and the older woman appear a little indignant
- the background stripes and the quote are missing
- instead there is a reference to four Oscar nominations
- the German subheading is different from the English one

Interpretation:
- Juno = probably name of the pregnant girl
- looks quite confident but not really happy:
→ pregnancy is probably unwanted but maybe not a total disaster for her life
- boy most likely the baby's father
- he seems more confused about the situation and their future than the girl
- both are not typical American blockbuster characters:
→ girl: not a typical girlie type
→ boy: does sports but doesn't look athletic
- maybe together because they are both outsiders and have to cope with the mockery of the in-crowd
- English poster suggests a comedy with funny dialogues, which is supported by the pun in the subheading
- the German poster shows two couples in the background (the older couple might be the girl's parents)
  → mother: unhappy about the pregnancy
  → father: seems to be confident
  → younger couple might not be the boy's parents
  → German subheading suggests that the girl seems to feel rather indifferent about her pregnancy
- subheading is less funny than the one on the English poster

Appeal:
- English poster is appealing because testimonial and subheading stress the fact that it is a comedy and has funny dialogues.
- German poster is appealing because it makes you curious to find out why the girl's pregancy does not worry her and who the other people are.

Methode
Nach der Einstimmung anhand der Filmplakate wird nun der Film gezeigt. Je nach Jahrgangsstufe und Erfahrungen der Schülerinnen und Schüler im Anschauen englischsprachiger Filme sollte der Film gegebenenfalls mit Untertiteln gezeigt werden. Natürlich kann an dieser Stelle beliebig viel Zeit auf die Filmanalyse verwandt werden, mit einer Vielzahl von Unterbrechungen, Szenenanalysen, Vorhersagen über den weiteren Handlungsverlauf, kreativen Arbeitsaufträgen etc. Es hat sich jedoch gezeigt, dass die Schülerinnen und Schüler im Allgemeinen wenig Motivation zeigen, das Thema Teenager Schwangerschaft erneut im Detail zu besprechen. Daher wird der Film hier lediglich als Ergänzung zur Lektüre betrachtet.

45

II. Modul 7

Mithilfe von **KV 19.1 – 19.3** erstellen die Schülerinnen und Schüler eine *guided summary*. Die Dialogtexte stammen aus Schlüsselszenen und erzählen somit die wesentlichen Etappen der Handlung. Indem die Lernenden ihren Kontext beschreiben, konstruieren sie wesentliche Elemente der Handlung.

Die Benennung der Gefühle der dargestellten Personen erfordert einen Perspektivwechsel, der den Lernenden weitere Ebenen des Films eröffnet.

Die Schülerinnen und Schüler lesen zunächst den Arbeitsauftrag auf **KV 19.1** während die Lehrkraft die Filmvorführung vorbereitet, so dass jeder weiß, auf was während des Anschauens zu achten ist. Als *pre-viewing* Aufgabe bringen die Lernenden die Dialoge in die von ihnen antizipierte Reihenfolge, welche beim Anschauen des Films überprüft wird. So werden die Lernenden nicht nur auf die Handlung neugierig, sondern setzen sich aktiver mit dem Film auseinander. Die Lehrkraft sollte zwischendurch hier und da den Film kurz anhalten, um den Schülerinnen und Schülern Zeit für das Ausfüllen der **KVs 19.1** bis **19.3** zu geben. Die Auswertung der Aufgaben erfolgt im Unterrichtsgespräch.

Ergebnis

1G – All three pregnancy tests positive
Feelings: Anger, helplessness, disbelief, hope
Context: Juno cannot believe that she is pregnant, therefore she takes three pregnancy tests. But every time the outcome is positive. She goes home and phones her friend Leah to tell her.

2A – Telling the father, Paulie
Feelings: Arrogance, superiority, curiosity
Context: Juno has decided to have an abortion and now she informs Paulie about the pregnancy and her decision. Paulie is paralysed with shock and accepts everything Juno says. She seems a little disappointed. Nevertheless, she phones the abortion clinic and makes an appointment.

3I – At the abortion clinic
Feelings: Sadness, insecurity, responsibility
Context: When Juno comes to the clinic, a girl from her school is demonstrating against abortion. She tells her that the baby already has fingernails. In the waiting room, Juno's former determination falters when she sees and hears the sound of fingernails all around her. She flees from the clinic.

4B– Meeting the adoptive parents
Feelings: apprehension, anxiety (father), happiness (Vanessa)
Context: Juno has found a nice couple to adopt the baby in the local newspaper and goes to meet them, accompanied by her father. Her parents are surprised with the situation but they cope well and promise their support.

5H – Jamming with Mark
Feelings: Surprise, affection, ease
Context: By coincidence, Juno and Mark find out that they share an interest in music and start a spontaneous jam session. The connection they feel helps Juno with her decision to sign the contract to give them her baby when it is born.

6C – The ultrasound photo
Feelings: Warmth, affection, happiness
Context: Juno refuses Paulie's offer to accompany her to the ultrasound
examination and takes Leah and her stepmother instead. It cheers her
up to hear the baby is healthy.

7D – Discussing Paulie's prom date
Feelings: Bewilderment, anger, surprise, jealousy
Context: After refusing Paulie, who stills loves Juno and would like to have a
relationship with her, she suggests to him that he should go to the prom
with a classmate. When she hears that he's going out with that girl, Juno
is jealous. She realizes that she likes Paulie more than she thought and
takes Paulie to task for going out with a girl he does not even like. Paulie
denies that and calls her immature.

8F – Dancing with Mark/ Mark's confession
Feelings: Affection (both), anger, confusion, shock
Context: Juno goes to bring Mark some CDs. He gives her a comic about a
pregnant super hero and they start dancing to the songs that remind
Mark of his prom. He confesses that he will leave Vanessa because he
does not want to be a father or to be married but wants to work on his
music career. Juno is mad at him and runs away.

9E – The baby is born
Feelings: Sadness, emptiness, love (both), security
Context: Juno has decided that she wants to give the baby to Vanessa anyway
after she has seen her with a little girl in a shopping mall. She also
realizes that she loves Paulie and tells him. Paulie comes to the hospital
to stand by her as soon as he finds out that Juno has given birth to the
baby.

Methode
Nachdem die SuS den Film gesehen haben, berichten sie in der folgenden Stunde,
inwieweit ihre vorherigen Erwartungen an Thema, Ablauf und Stil des Films erfüllt
oder nicht erfüllt worden sind.

Danach bietet es sich an, die Geschichten, die im Roman und im Film erzählt
werden, zu vergleichen.

Als weiteres Thema könnten die SuS versuchen, sich kritisch mit der Realitätsnähe
beider Geschichten auseinanderzusetzen.

Abschließend sollten die SuS begründete Statements darüber abgeben, ob Ihnen
das Buch oder der Film besser gefallen hat.

Fragestellung
*To what extent are both stories about teenage pregnancies ("Juno" and "Slam")
comparable?*

Ergebnis

Juno	Slam
teenage girl's point of view	teenage boy's point of view
girl initiates the sex	girl initiates the sex
girl decides what to do about the baby, boy has no say in the matter	girl decides what to do about the baby, boy has no say in the matter
the baby's father's hobby is sport (track running)	the baby's father's hobby is sport (skating)
Paulie is a nerd	Sam is cool and has friends
Juno is confident and independent-minded (outward appearance, behavior, taste in music etc.)	Alicia is a girlie and absolutely mainstream
Paulie's mother is against their relationship	Sam's mother is against their relationship
the baby is given up for adoption	they keep the baby
…	…

Fragestellung
Which of the stories is more realistic?

Ergebnis
Both book and film are not entirely realistic:
- Juno is not a typical 16-year-old, she is far too laid back about the situation, even though she shows slight traces of weakness or insecurity once in a while.
- Sam is whizzed into the future to get an insight into how his life might turn out.

Methode
Als Hausaufgabe nehmen die Schülerinnen und Schüler einen Perspektivwechsel vor und beschreiben die Schwangerschaft Junos aus Paulies Sicht. Auch wenn Paulie Sam aus dem Roman nur wenig ähnelt, können hier Erkenntnisse aus der Lektüre eingebracht werden und die Gefühle und Gedanken eines minderjährigen Vaters antizipiert werden, der von der werdenden Mutter mehr oder weniger ausgeschlossen wird – eine Situation, die sich Sam sicherlich an dem ein oder anderen Punkt gewünscht hätte.

Aufgabe
Imagine the story of the film being told from Paulie's point of view and he was speaking the voice-over in the movie. Consider the following questions:
- How does he experience the situation?
- How does he feel when Juno tells him that she is pregnant and wants to have an abortion?
- What does he think when he finds out that Juno will keep the baby and give it up for adoption?
- What is going on in his head when he feels totally left out?

Musterlösung

That morning, when I stepped out the door to do my usual running exercise, Juno was sitting there … in an armchair, smoking a pipe, with a carpet and a whole set of living room furnishings. That girl is so weird! She looked at me and told me that she was pregnant without even blinking. God, she scared the shit out of me! We only had sex this one time and now she was pregnant! I was going to be a … But I had no time to think further because Juno told me straight away that she was going to have an abortion if that was fine with me. Come on, what could I say but that it was OK. If Juno has made her mind up about something, nothing can stop her anyway, least of all me. But did she really expect me to refuse?

We hardly talked after that, not at school and she hardly came over to my house anymore. She only told me in passing one day that she was giving the baby up for adoption. Did she think I was not interested in that fact? But as always, stubborn Juno probably wanted to do this alone. I missed her a lot. I mean, she was not only my best friend, I was also still in love with her.

Juno became rounder and rounder and everybody started talking about her pregnancy at school and they soon also started talking about me. I did not care much about that. I mean, Juno is the coolest girl in the whole school, why would I be embarrassed? Instead I started taking my track running even more seriously than before. Then, one evening, Juno came over to my house. She went on about that Mark guy, who is going to adopt the baby, and I had to tell her that I wanted to be with her again. Gosh, what a snub she gave me when she didn't even react but talked about me going to the prom with Katrina Devoort.

Then one day, when I had actually asked Katrina out to the prom – it had turned out she was not that terrible after all – Juno came over to me in a break and started ranting how much she detested me for inviting Katrina and her having better things to do than going to the prom, yada yada yada… I was confused. First she wants me to ask Katrina, now she hates me for it. Must have been the hormones, I thought. But it turned out that she was just jealous. Boy, was I happy when I stepped out the door for my running exercise one morning and found our mailbox full of my favourite tic tacs. I knew they must be from Juno and when she caught me at the sports field to tell me that she loved me, we kissed. I was the happiest person on earth!!!

She didn't talk about the baby or about what was going on inside her head but I knew that to be there for her was the least I could do. And when Juno wasn't there when I won the track race, I knew she must have gone into labour. I wasn't mad at her for not informing me. That's just how she is. I ran to the hospital as fast as I could and found her in a state in which I had never seen her before. She was lying in bed, crying, sad and totally vulnerable. I could only imagine that she must feel some kind of emptiness now that the baby was not inside of her anymore. I knew she would not talk about her feelings – she hardly ever does – so I lay beside her and just held her close. We never talk about the pregnancy or the baby but Juno makes sure we use contraceptives.

II.   Modul 8

Methode
Als Abschluss der Filmbesprechung lesen die Schülerinnen und Schüler eine deutschsprachige Filmkritik (**KV 20**). Der einfach herzuleitende situative Kontext – die Schule hat eine englischsprachige Schülerzeitung – bietet einen realistischen Rahmen für eine Sprachmittlung. Falls die Schülerinnen und Schüler mit dem Aufgabenformat noch nicht vertraut sind, sollte zunächst geklärt werden, dass es sich bei einer Mediation nicht um eine Übersetzung handelt. Strategien zur Vorgehensweise finden die Lernenden auf **KV 20**. Zur Besprechung der Ergebnisse ist es hilfreich, die Mediation eines Schülers zu kopieren und im Detail zu besprechen. Anhand dessen können effektiv über inhaltliche Aspekte sowie sprachliche Gestaltung der Lösung gesprochen werden und Verbesserungsvorschläge direkt eingebaut werden. Auch auf die typische Falle – Sätze werden Wort für Wort und damit unidiomatisch und häufig grammatikalisch falsch übersetzt – muss unbedingt hingewiesen werden.

Im zweiten Teil der Aufgabe bekommen die Schülerinnen und Schüler die Gelegenheit, ihre eigene Meinung zum Film zu äußern. Bei der Besprechung der Aufgabe sollte darauf geachtet werden, dass der Bezug zur *review* gegeben ist.

Fragestellung
Do you find the review fair and accurate?

Ergebnis
The review "Pregnant and having fun" of the film "Juno" praises the director's talent in once more turning a serious subject into a comedy. Juno is a cheeky 16-year-old who becomes pregnant after having sex for the first time with her slightly inhibited friend. After visiting an abortion clinic, she decides to give the baby up for adoption. She finds a rich couple from the suburbs who want to adopt the child and Juno soon interferes in their pedantic and predictable life.

The author says that the movie is not a conventional Hollywood drama with big emotions but a comedy with witty dialogues. The movie's strong points are its biting wit and mocking observations of everyday life and the characters. But sometimes exactly this is a little overdone and some scenes and minor characters lose credibility. Occasionally, a softer note would have been more suitable.

Modul 8   Creating a film trailer for *Slam* (4 Std.)

Lernziel
Die Schlüsselszenen aus "Slam" bestimmen, Kenntnisse der Filmgestaltung gewinnen und anwenden.

Methode
Die Arbeit mit Filmen erweist sich immer wieder als motivationsfördernd. Die im Folgenden beschriebene Unterrichtseinheit kann sowohl im Anschluss an Modul 7 als auch unabhängig von der Arbeit mit dem Film *Juno* eingesetzt werden.

Die Schülerinnen und Schüler sollten zunächst gemeinsam einen Filmtrailer anschauen, um anhand dessen die Kriterien für die Erstellung eines Trailers zu sammeln. Möglich wäre hier natürlich der Einsatz des *Juno*-Trailers

http://www.youtube.com/watch?v=K0SKf0K3bxg, aber auch jeder andere Trailer ist
ebenso zweckdienlich. Die Ergebnisse werden an der Tafel gesammelt, da die
Schülerinnen und Schüler bei der Entwicklung eines Trailers zu „Slam" darauf
zurückgreifen sollen.

Fragestellung
What are the criteria for a good film trailer?

Ergebnis
- main aspects of the story line are introduced
- the ending of the film is not given away
- it must make you curious about the movie and inspire you to want to watch it
- the title, probably the cast and the director's name, and the release date must
  be given
- typical/especially funny or exciting scenes are included
- many cuts between film scenes
- in action-packed movies many filming techniques are presented

Methode
Im Anschluss beschäftigen sich die Schülerinnen und Schüler mit Filmtechniken,
deren Funktionsweise sowie den dazugehörigen Fachtermini. Dazu werden
zunächst anhand von **KV 21.1/21.2** die Fachtermini vorgestellt, angewandt und
dadurch gefestigt. Da es hier kein richtig oder falsch bei der Wahl der
Kameraeinstellung gibt, ist das unten stehende Ergebnis lediglich als Vorschlag zu
betrachten. Die Schülerinnen und Schüler überlegen erst in Einzelarbeit, welche
Kameraeinstellung sie wählen würden, um die gegebenen Szenerien darzustellen.
In einer anschließenden Partnerarbeit tauschen sie sich mit einem Mitschüler aus
und begründen ihre Wahl der Kameraeinstellung.

Ergebnis
- raindrops on a window:
  close-up – extreme close-up, eye-level, zooming in while a raindrop is running
  down the window
- couple sitting at a table:
  long shot, eye-level, zooming in on their faces
- petal of a beautiful flower:
  close-up, high-angle, zooming out
- full moon:
  long shot, low-angle
- boy and girl kissing:
  medium shot, eye-level, panning a full circle around them
- people crossing a street:
  long shot, eye-level, camera follows them with a pan
- a child crying:
  medium shot, high-angle, zooming in
- a diamond:
  extreme close-up, high-angle
- an ice skater:
  long shot, eye-level, panning

II.   Modul 8

- woman on the phone:
  close shot, eye-level
- neighbours talking over the fence:
  long shot, eye-level
- happiness:
  close-up
- football that is kicked the whole length of a pitch: long shot, high-angle,
  panning

Methode

Da die Vorstellungskraft der Schülerinnen und Schüler, welche Kameraeinstellung
welche Wirkung erzielt, oft sehr unterschiedlich ist, sollte man sich die Zeit
nehmen, in Kleingruppen von bis zu sechs Lernenden dies praktisch zu erproben.
Die Schülerinnen und Schüler sollen dazu verschiedene Gefühle nicht durch
herausragendes schauspielerisches Talent, sondern durch eine geeignete
Kameraeinstellung darstellen (siehe **KV 22**). Die Gruppen werden hierzu jeweils mit
einer Digitalkamera ausgestattet. (Sollte man die Schülerinnen und Schüler selbst
Kameras von zu Hause mitbringen lassen, muss man unbedingt auch an das
Transferkabel zum Computer erinnern!) Beim Ausprobieren werden die Lernenden
schnell merken, dass beispielsweise ein low-angle shot eine Person bedrohlich
oder ein high-angle shot eine Person zerbrechlich wirken lassen kann.

Die Fotos werden auf den Computer transferiert und per Beamer angeschaut.
Dabei kann man die Ergebnisse der Gruppen am besten vergleichen, wenn man
zunächst jeweils eine Stimmung von allen Gruppen betrachtet und die erzielten
Wirkungen der Kameraeinstellungen analysiert. Evtl. kann man über das
wirkungsvollste Foto anstimmen lassen und bestimmte Wirkungsweisen (z.B.
A low-angle shot makes a person appear bigger.) an der Tafel zur Sicherung
festhalten.

Im Anschluss erstellen die Gruppen (es können auch neue Gruppen gebildet
werden) ein *Storyboard* für einen Trailer zu *Slam*. Die Überlegungen dazu basieren
auf den gewonnenen Erkenntnissen bezüglich Kameraeinstellungen und Aufbau
eines Filmtrailers. **KV 23** dient lediglich als Vorlage, acht oder neun Bilder werden
jedoch im Allgemeinen nicht ausreichen. Je nach Arbeitseinstellung der Klasse
sollte man ein oberes oder unteres Limit setzen (10-15 Bilder). Die Präsentation der
Ergebnisse kann je nach technischer Ausstattung auf unterschiedliche Art und
Weise geschehen, z.B. die Storyboards werden eingescannt und per Beamer
präsentiert, die Storyboards werden auf Folie kopiert und per OHP präsentiert, die
Storyboards werden auf Gruppentischen ausgelegt und die Schülerinnen und
Schüler gehen im Klassenraum in Kleingruppen von Tisch zu Tisch und bekommen
von jeweils einem Verantwortlichen die Ergebnisse präsentiert. Zur situativen
Einbettung der Aufgabe könnte die Lehrkraft als Auftraggeber (Filmfirma) dienen,
die am Ende der Präsentationen dem überzeugendsten Vorschlag den Zuschlag
gibt. Bei der Präsentation sollten die Gruppen ihre Bilder beschreiben und erklären,
was sie sich dabei gedacht haben.

II.   Modul 9

Modul 9   Ideensammlung weiterer *activities*

Die Sammlung weiterer Unterrichtsideen zur Arbeit im Anschluss an die Lektüre
hat lediglich Vorschlagscharakter. Auf eine Beschreibung eines dezidierten
methodischen Vorgehens wird an dieser Stelle verzichtet. Viele der vorgestellten
Ideen können als Zusatzleistungen für Schülerinnen und Schüler benutzt werden.
Eine inhaltliche Besprechung der Ergebnisse ist oft nicht nötig, da es sich um
kreative Gestaltungsaufgaben handelt.

Soundtrack zum Roman gestalten

Viele Schülerinnen und Schüler sind sehr musikinteressiert und haben selten die
Gelegenheit, ihre Kenntnisse über Popmusik und/oder Bands im Unterricht
einzusetzen. Die Aufgabe, einen Soundtrack zum Roman zu erstellen und evtl. auch
künstlerisch zu gestalten, dürfte daher bei vielen auf Interesse stoßen. Dabei
können nicht nur Songs über *teenage pregnancy* (siehe Klausur 1) oder *Skating*
genutzt werden, sondern z.B. auch Songs, die bestimmte Stimmungen ausdrücken.
Bei der Gestaltung des CD-Booklets sollen die Schülerinnen und Schüler jeweils die
Szene beschreiben und erläutern, warum sie eine bestimmte Songauswahl für
diese Szene getroffen haben.

Designen eines neuen Buch Covers/Poster eines persönlichen Helden

Diese Aufgabe richtet sich besonders an künstlerisch begabte Schülerinnen und
Schüler, den anderen dürfte diese Aufgabe wenig Spaß machen. Im Internetauftritt
von Spinebreakers, einer Art virtuellem Leseclub, kann man sogar an einem
Wettbewerb zur Gestaltung eines Posters seines persönlichen Helden teilnehmen.

http://www.spinebreakers.co.uk/Creative/Pages/gedged.aspx

Präsentationen (Skating, Tony Hawk, Teenage pregnancy in the USA)

Einige Schüler sind möglicherweise selbst Skater oder Fans von Tony Hawk und
können hier ihr Expertenwissen einbringen.

Eggbert: Sich um ein "Baby" kümmern

Dieses Projekt kennt man aus zahlreichen amerikanischen Teenie-Filmen, da dies
offensichtlich ein typischer Bestandteil der amerikanischen *health care classes* ist.
Im Allgemeinen gehen zwei Lernende als Paar zusammen und bekommen ein Ei
als Babyersatz, um das sie sich über einen bestimmten Zeitraum hinweg kümmern
müssen. Meist werden gemischtgeschlechtliche Paare gebildet, wenn das in der
Lerngruppe nicht aufgeht, gibt es auch homosexuelle Paare oder Alleinerziehende.
Das Ei muss dabei wie ein Baby behandelt werden, d.h. es darf nicht allein gelassen
werden, in eine Kiste gestopft oder über eine längere Zeit unbeobachtet gelassen
werden. Wie die Elternpaare sich die Betreuungszeit einteilen, ist ihnen überlassen.
Bei der Auswertung wird überprüft, welches Ei überlebt hat und die Schülerinnen
und Schüler berichten aus ihren Erfahrungen als Eltern.

Spielen der Lieblingsszenen

In Kleingruppen spielen die Schülerinnen und Schüler ihre Lieblingsszenen aus
dem Roman nach. Dazu müssen sie nicht nur einen Prosatext in ein *play script*
umwandeln, sondern sich besonders Gedanken um die Darstellung der Charaktere

II. Klausuren

machen. Dies erfordert erneut einen Perspektivenwechsel und ermöglicht einen vertieften Zugang zum Text.

Brief an Nick Hornby

Im Allgemeinen bleiben nach der Lektüre eines Romans immer Fragen offen, die man als Leser eigentlich gerne beantwortet haben möchte, z.B. wie kam der Autor auf die Zukunftsvisionen als literarisches Mittel etc. Diese Fragen könnten gesammelt und zusammen mit den persönlichen Meinungen der Schülerinnen und Schüler über den Roman an Nick Hornby bzw. an seinen Verlag geschickt werden (siehe http://www.penguin.co.uk/static/cs/uk/0/minisites/nickhornby/index.html). Wenn man Glück hat, bekommt man sogar eine Antwort.

Klausuren

Klausur A

Der Klausurvorschlag bezieht sich auf den ganzen Roman und sollte erst nach der kompletten Lektüre eingesetzt werden. Der Song muss nicht zwangsläufig während der Klausur angehört werden, kann aber beispielsweise bei ihrer Besprechung zum Einsatz kommen.

Weitere Songs, die das Thema *teenage pregnancy* behandeln, könnten zur vertiefenden Analyse und zum Vergleich bearbeitet werden.

Beispiele:
Madonna – Papa don't preach
Kenny Chesney – There goes my life
Tupac – Brenda's got a baby
Fantasia Barrino – Baby Mama
Elvis Presley – In the ghetto
Kamary Phillips – Five minutes

Erwartungshorizont
Songwriter:
- he has just heard that he is going to be a father
- he knows his life is going to change
- he begins to pray => to thank God or to ask God for support
- he is happy, sheds tears of joy
- he welcomes his son "with arms wide open" and looks forward to showing him everything
- he does not know if he is ready to be the man he has to be
- but he will go through this with his wife/ girlfriend
- he hopes that his son will not be like him and that he understands that he can take control of his life

Sam:
- also knows that his life is going to change
- in the beginning he is not happy at all => he runs away
- later, after having been whizzed into the future, he can look forward to meeting his son

54

- he does not pray but asks TH for help
- he also knows that he is not ready to be the man he has to be, he is still immature
- Sam and Alicia are much more down to earth and more scared => don't stand in awe that they have created life
- Sam does not mention if he wants Roof to be like him or Alicia
- but he wants his son to get a good education unlike the people in his family had
- being whizzed into the future has helped Sam to see that his life wouldn't be as bad as he expected it to be:
- he can go to school
- he can handle Roof
- he will have a nice girlfriend
- Alicia will be alright
- TH was always there for him when he could not talk to other people
- he always, more or less, helped Sam with his answers

Klausur B

Der Klausurvorschlag kann zu jedem beliebigen Zeitpunkt nach der Lektüre von Kapitel 11 eingesetzt werden. Bei der Besprechung der Klausur lohnt es sich, ein kurzes Video-Interview mit Alphie und Chantelle zu zeigen, welches den Wahnsinn der Situation noch einmal hervorhebt.

Siehe http://www.thesun.co.uk/sol/homepage/news/article2233878.ece

Erwartungshorizont
Summary:
- topic sentence: article "Baby-faced boy Alfie Patten is father at 13" by Lucy Hagan, published on 13 Feb 2009 in The Sun deals with the story of a teenage couple who have become parents at the ages of 13 and 15 and who do not know yet how to handle the situation
- Alfie tells the reporter that their daughter Maisie was conceived after he and his girlfriend Chantelle had a single night of unprotected sex
- they found out about the baby when C. was 12 weeks pregnant and kept it a secret for the following six weeks because they were too scared to tell their parents
- they had decided against an abortion because they thought having a baby would be a nice experience
- after their release from the hospital, Chantelle and Maisie are living with Chantelle's family while Alfie is still living with his mother but is spending most of his time at the Steadmans' house and is allowed to stay overnight
- they have to rely on the financial support of both families as they still go to school and earn no money
- Alfie's father thinks his son is scared about the future and is a typical 13-year-old, as he is still unaware what being a parent means for him

II. Klausuren

Sam's letter to Alphie:
- Alphie is 3 years younger than Sam
- in both cases their girlfriends became pregnant the first time they have unprotected sex
- both lose their virginity to the mothers of their children
- both do not really know how to deal with the situation
- it seems as if Alphie wants the baby whereas Sam doesn't
- after telling Sam, Alicia immediately tells her parents and Sam's mother about the pregnancy whereas Alphie and Chantelle wait until it is too late for an abortion
- Sam's mother is a single parent, too
- Alicia's family is financially well off whereas Chantelle's family lives on benefits
- Alphie knows he will be a great father, Sam has doubts about his job as a father

advice: ad lib

Klausur C

Der Klausurvorschlag bezieht sich nicht auf die Lektüre direkt, sondern eher auf die Statistiken und Hintergrundinformationen zum Thema *teenage pregnancy*. Hintergrundwissen in diesem Gebiet wird dementsprechend vorausgesetzt. Vom Aufgabenformat und dem Sprachniveau des Zeitungsartikels her sollte dieser Vorschlag erst in der Oberstufe eingesetzt werden. Zeitumfang: 3 Unterrichtsstunden.

Erwartungshorizont
Summary:
- topic sentence: newspaper article "Rap music blamed for teen pregnancy" by Shaun Bailey, published on 23 August 2006 in the Daily Mail deals with the influence that the portrayal of gender roles in rap music has on the sexual attitudes of teenagers
- a study by a leading health care organisation in the US has shown that there is a connection between the music teenagers listen to and their sexual behaviour and attitudes
- the study says that teenagers who listen to music that degrades women, making them into sexual objects and depicts men as insatiable studs, progress more quickly in their sexual behaviour than teenagers who prefer different kinds of music
- consequences are earlier sexual activity, leading to a spread of disease and underage pregnancy, and a change in the sexual self-image of boys and girls (girls accept a submissive role, boys take on a reckless sexual behaviour)
- the study recommends that parents get involved in their children's musical habits and talk to them about the content of the music they listen to

Discussion of quote:

pro:
- the article from the Daily Mail supports the view that sex should be 'kept away' from young people
- if sex was not displayed openly in all kinds of areas in life, children would be less curious to have sex themselves
- if children are older when they have first sexual intercourse, they will deal with it in a much more responsible way, therefore the teenage pregnancy rates will decrease
- if it became 'trendy' to wait, teenagers would do so
- …

con:
- statistics show that the problem of a high teenage pregnancy rate in the UK has existed for more than 20 years and rap music as well as music television were only made popular within the last two decades
- speaking openly about sex and introducing sex education at schools are only answers to a problem that has existed before
- teenagers are curious about sex even if teachers and parents do not talk about it, they will still have sex in secret without any knowledge of contraception and sexually transmitted diseases
- keeping sex away from children would mean the introduction of a strict system of censorship which is against human rights
- …

Kopiervorlage 1.1

Group 1: The cover

Task: Describe the book cover, make a connection to the title and predict what the novel might be about. Use your imagination to tell the story or to ask questions.

Useful phrases:

The novel/book/story might be about … .

It may tell the story of … .

The story probably focuses on … .

It will possibly centre on/around … .

The story will revolve around … .

The book might deal with … .

The cover suggests that … .

The title may hint at … .

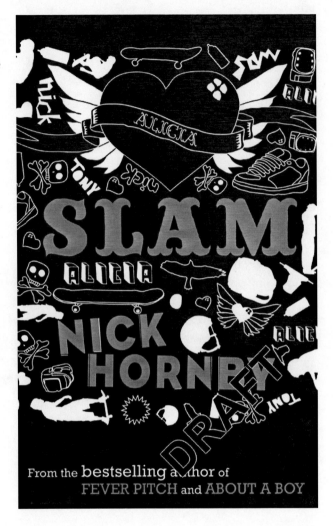

Kopiervorlage 1.2

Group 2: The blurb

Task: Read the blurb of the novel (see below) and summarize it in your own words. Make a connection to the title and predict what the book might be about. Especially focus on the "little accident" that happens to Sam. Use your imagination to tell the story or to ask questions.

'There was this time when everything seemed to have come together. And so obviously it was time to go and screw it all up.'

Sam is sixteen and a skater. Just so there are no terrible misunderstandings: skating = skateboarding. There's no ice. Life is ticking along nicely for Sam: his mum's got rid of her rubbish boyfriend, he's thinking about college and he's met someone. Alicia.

Then a little accident happens. One with big consequences for someone just finding his way in life. Sam can't run (let alone skate) away from this one. He's a boy facing a man's problems and the question is – has he got what it takes to confront them?

Useful phrases:

The novel/book/story might be about … .

It may tell the story of … .

The story probably focuses on … .

It will possibly centre on/around … .

The story will revolve around … .

The book might deal with … .

The cover suggests that … .

The title may hint at … .

2

Kopiervorlage 2: Sam's character file

Task: After reading the first chapter of SLAM fill in Sam's character file below. Use all the information you can find.

Name	
Age	
Family situation	
School performance	
Leisure time activities	
Idols	
Thoughts about life	
Additional information	

© Ernst Klett Sprachen GmbH, Stuttgart 2009 | www.klett.de | Alle Rechte vorbehalten
Von dieser Druckvorlage ist die Vervielfältigung für den eigenen Unterrichtsgebrauch gestattet.
Die Kopiergebühren sind abgegolten.

Kopiervorlage 3:   Love is...

You probably all know the "Love is ..." cartoons from newspapers. They always show the little nude couple and make some statement about what love is (see example on the right).

Task: Take a look at the cartoon below and add a suitable statement about love.

...feeling his love all around you.

Kopiervorlage 4: Love?

Below you will find some proverbs, sayings and popular beliefs about love and sex.

Task: According to what you have read so far, would Sam and Alicia agree or disagree with these? Indicate with different coloured crosses (Alicia – red, Sam – blue) where you see them.

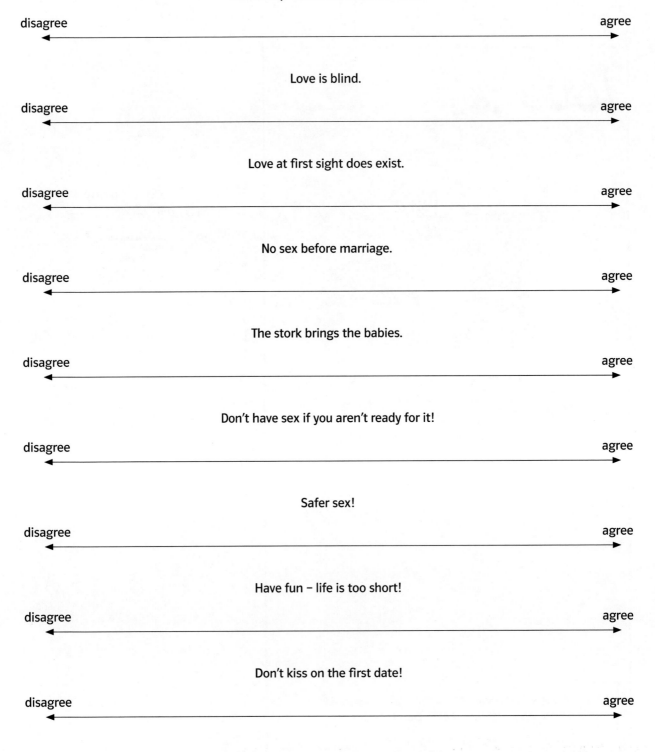

Friendship has to come before sex.

disagree ←—————————————————————→ agree

Love is blind.

disagree ←—————————————————————→ agree

Love at first sight does exist.

disagree ←—————————————————————→ agree

No sex before marriage.

disagree ←—————————————————————→ agree

The stork brings the babies.

disagree ←—————————————————————→ agree

Don't have sex if you aren't ready for it!

disagree ←—————————————————————→ agree

Safer sex!

disagree ←—————————————————————→ agree

Have fun – life is too short!

disagree ←—————————————————————→ agree

Don't kiss on the first date!

disagree ←—————————————————————→ agree

Kopiervorlage 5:   Vocabulary "Dating and love"

adoration	great love and devotion
advances	attempts to start a romantic relationship
affair	temporary romantic relationship
affection	warmth, liking
beloved	greatly loved person
to break a heart	to reject or wound one's lover
brokenhearted	rejected in love
to cheat	to deceive one's lover with another, secret lover
commitment	bond of love and responsibility
couple	two people who are in love with each other
crush	temporary intense feeling of love
to fancy sb	to be attracted to sb
fling	a short love affair
French kiss	deep kiss with tongue inserted in the partner's mouth
going steady	regularly dating one person
head over heels in love	very much in love
hug (to hug)	enthusiastic, affectionate embrace
jealousy	resentment caused by a real or imagined rival
to lose one's heart	to fall in love
love at first sight	immediate attraction
lovesick	emotionally unbalanced from love
to make out	to kiss and fondle passionately for extended time
obsession	mania, extreme fascination
passion	strong emotional response to lover
puppy love	youthful, immature love
reconciliation (to reconcile)	settlement of differences with one's lover
relationship	involvement of two persons being in love
romance	love affair
seduction (to seduce)	persuading s.b. into having sex
to toy with	to play at love with no commitment
true	faithful
unfaithful	betraying a lover
unrequited love	love for someone who does not love in return

© Ernst Klett Sprachen GmbH, Stuttgart 2009 | www.klett.de | Alle Rechte vorbehalten
Von dieser Druckvorlage ist die Vervielfältigung für den eigenen Unterrichtsgebrauch gestattet.
Die Kopiergebühren sind abgegolten.

Kopiervorlage 6: Sex, pregnancy and birth

Task: Connect verbs and nouns/adjectives to form meaningful expressions and visualize the connection between these expressions in a flow chart. The verbs do not always come first.

---

verbs

to use	to have (4x)	to go for	to terminate	to suffer (from)
to miss	to make	to father *(zeugen)*	to expect	to deliver
to consult *(befragen, hinzuziehen)*	to be (4x)	to conceive *(empfangen)*		to grow
to be overdue *(überfällig)*	to keep	to give birth to	to be born	to make

---

nouns/ adjectives

love	a baby (2x)	pregnant	a pregnancy test	a child (3x)
midwife *(Hebamme)*	a contraceptive		a miscarriage *(Fehlgeburt)*	
the pregnancy	on the pill	one's period	pregnancy symptoms	the embryo
the period	nausea *(Übelkeit)*	an abortion		by Caesarean section
a gynaecologist	nauseous	sex	the doctor	the baby (3x)
a scan	a doctor	sick		a condom

Kopiervorlage 7.1: There are choices to make ...

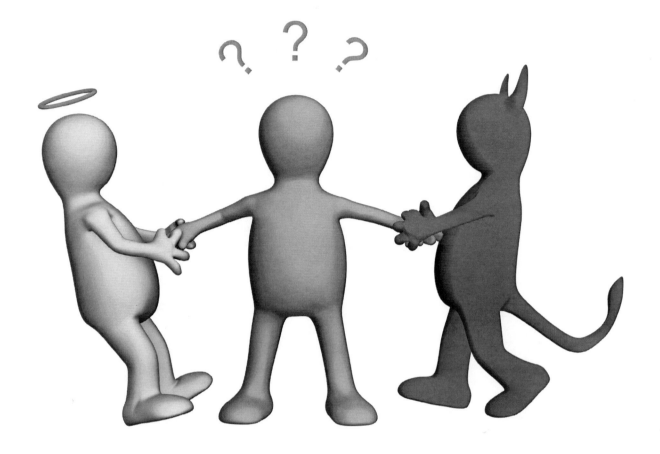

Shall I tell Sam that I am pregnant?

Kopiervorlage 7.2: There are choices to make ...

Shall I have an abortion?

Kopiervorlage 7.3: There are choices to make …

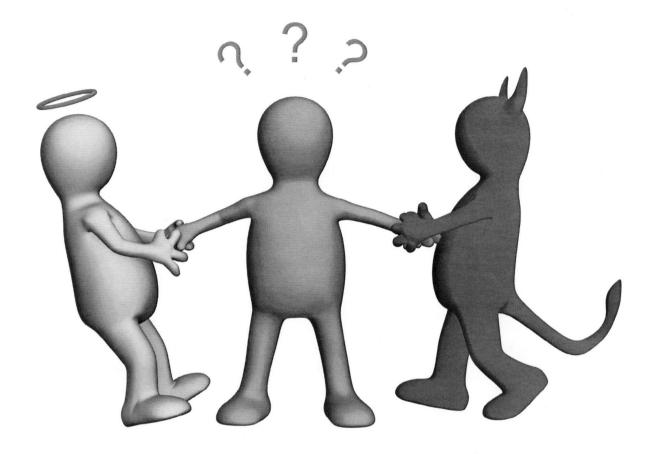

Shall I give the baby up for adoption?

Kopiervorlage 7.4: There are choices to make ...

Shall I raise the child on my own?

Kopiervorlage 7.5: There are choices to make ...

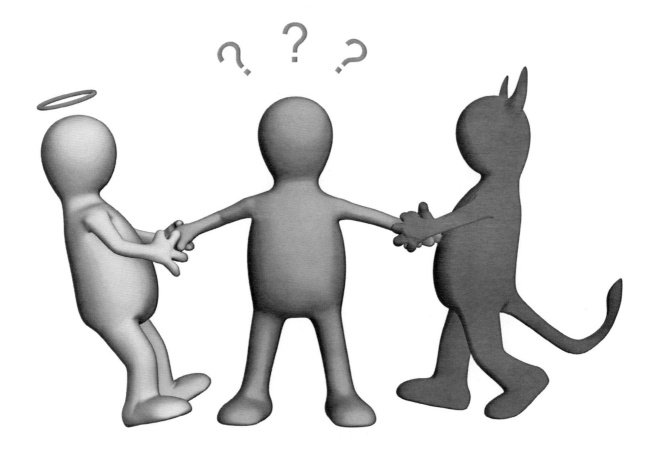

Shall I raise the child together with Sam?

Kopiervorlage 8: The parents' reactions

The following quotations from chapter nine show the reactions to Alicia's pregnancy from both her parents and Sam's mother.

> "Here's a good way of not getting someone pregnant: Don't have sex with them."

> "Do you hate us? Is that what this is about?"

> "Thirty-two. So she was sixteen when you were born ... Jesus Christ. Don't you people ever learn anything?"

> "How did this happen? I presumed you were having sex. I didn't think you were too stupid to use contraception."

> "Of all the things you could do. All the ways you could hurt me."

Tasks:

a) Find out who said what to whom and describe the situation in which it is said.

b) Try and explain the thoughts and feelings each person wants to express with his/her statement.

c) Write an inner monologue for either of the three where they reflect on their feelings a bit further. Take your results from b) into account.

Kopiervorlage 9: Learning to cope with pregnancy

Chapter 10:

In chapter 10, Sam reports about the next few weeks after telling their parents that Alicia was pregnant. Put the sentences below into the right order and add sentences where necessary to make a concise summary of the chapter.

1. They go to a maternity class and feel out of place because the other parents-to-be are much older. ☐

2. They kiss on the way home and decide to get back together, but don't have a sexual relationship anymore. ☐

3. His mum tells his father about the pregnancy. He takes it lightly and with humour. ☐

4. Mark moves in with Sam and his mother. ☐

5. Sam and Alicia go to a scan and find out the baby is a boy. ☐

6. They find out about it at school and surprisingly even the teachers are interested as they want to try out a new programme for teenage parents. ☐

Chapter 11:

Spot the mistakes in the following summary of chapter 11. Underline and correct them.

Alicia's parents think that Sam enriched their daughter's life, so they make an effort to be nice, which means they keep on talking about skating. They consider Sam part of their family now and so they are happy that Sam and Alicia want to live together in Sam's mother's house when the baby is born and accept this. That night, Sam goes cycling for the first time in a while. His friend Rabbit tells him that he thinks Sam screwed up his life but Sam realizes how boring his life was before. When he comes home, Sam's mother tries to talk him out of marrying Alicia but after asking his father for advice, he shows responsibility.

Chapter 12:

Use the following keywords from chapter 12 to write a summary.

- future
- baby-sister
- phone call
- jab
- his son's proper name

- swings
- toyshop
- *Dressing Salad*
- seven

Answer the following questions:

1. Sam thinks TH is responsible for his being whizzed into the future. What do you think is the author's reason for introdroucing this kind of 'time travel'?

2. Sam asks his mother to give him marks out of ten for how he is doing. How many points would you give him? Why?

© Ernst Klett Sprachen GmbH, Stuttgart 2009 | www.klett.de | Alle Rechte vorbehalten
Von dieser Druckvorlage ist die Vervielfältigung für den eigenen Unterrichtsgebrauch gestattet.
Die Kopiergebühren sind abgegolten.

Kopiervorlage 10: Ideas for checking reading comprehension

Task:

You deal with chapter _____ of *Slam*.

Use one of the task types below to check the rest of the class' comprehension of the chapter.

True/false sentences

Write some true and some wrong sentences about the chapter. Ask the class to find out whether they are true or false and let them correct the false ones.

Jumbled sentences

Pick out some (10) noteworthy sentences from the chapter. Mix them up. Ask the class to put them into the correct order.

Finish the sentences

Choose the beginnings of some sentences. Get your classmates to finish the sentences off.

Who said it?

Let the class find out the person who said a certain sentence from the novel.

(More difficult!) Who said it to whom, when, where and why?

Let the class find out the missing information about a certain quotation.

Key words

Choose some significant words from the chapter. Ask the class to put them into the context of the novel.

Flashlight Summary

Write down the first sentence of a summary of the chapter. Every student must add one sentence to the collective summary of the chapter.

What's wrong with it?

Prepare an inaccurate summary of the chapter. Let the class detect and correct the mistakes.

Kopiervorlage 11: Preventing teenage pregnancy

In 1998, Britain had the highest teenage pregnancy rate in Europe. The conceptions per 1000 women at an age between 15 and 17 was as high as 46.6. Therefore the government developed a Teenage Pregnancy Strategy which represents the first coordinated attempt to tackle both the causes and the consequences of teenage pregnancy.

The strategy's targets were:

- Halve the under-18 conception rate by 2010, and establish a firm downward trend in the under-16 rate.
- Increase the proportion of teenage parents in education, training or employment to 60% by 2010, to reduce their risk of long-term social exclusion.

The strategy is based on international research on what works to reduce teenage pregnancy and improve health/education outcomes for teenage parents and their children. The strategy has five main themes:

- Joint action
- National Media Campaign
- Support for the parents of teenagers
- Prevention including improving sex and relationship education and access to contraception
- Support for teenage parents

Task: Think about the five main themes of the strategy. What could each of them include? How do you evaluate their chances of helping to reduce teenage pregnancy?

	strategy might include	chances of helping to reduce teenage pregnancy (+++ = very good; --- = very small)
Joint action		
National Media Campaign		
Support for the parents of teenagers		
Prevention (including improving sex and relationship education and access to contraception)		
Support for teenage parents		

Kopiervorlage 12: Working with tables, graphs and charts

Introduction

What is the **topic** presented?
What **type of presentation** has been chosen?
What is its **source**?
What is its **time of publication**?
What **period of time** is covered or what **point of time** does it refer to?
What **figures** are presented – numbers or percentage figures?

> **Useful words and phrases**
>
> pie chart, bar chart, table, line graph
> The topic/ subject/ theme is …
> to provide information on
> to cover a period of … months/years
> to show the development over a period of time
> the bars indicate/ represent

Description and development

Which **extremes** and significant **changes** are presented?
Where are **similarities** and **differences**?
What is the **proportion** of individual numbers compared to the total number?

> **Useful words and phrases**
>
> almost no …/ most …/ only very few …
> less than …/ more than …
> a tiny minority of …/ the vast majority …
> roughly one out of four …/ over two thirds of …
> a third of the …/ half of the …
> a high/ low percentage of …
> highest/ lowest figure/ score
> in comparison with/ in contrast to
> to reach a peak/ a low point/ an all-time high/low … of more than five million
> to remain constant/ unchanged
> a sudden/ unexpected/ slight/ steep/ rapid/ gradual/ steady/ continual
> fall/ drop/ decrease/ decline/ increase/ rise/ growth
> to go up/ to grow/ to increase/ to rise/ to decrease/ to fall/ to drop
> unexpectedly/ sharply/ gradually/ steadily/ continually/ consistently by 2%

Analysis and evaluation

Which **conclusions** can you draw from the statistical evidence?
What **events, political situations, social conditions** etc. stand in connection to the subject presented or can account for the trends shown?

> **Useful words and phrases**
>
> to contrast/ to compare
> to show/ reveal/ represent/ indicate/ illustrate/ to prove
> one can conclude that …
> … can be explained by …

Kopiervorlage 13:   British national media campaigns

There are three national media campaigns to reduce teenage pregnancy:

'RU Thinking' is aimed at younger teenagers, promoting messages on delaying first sex and avoiding peer pressure.

'Want Respect? Use a Condom' is aimed at sexually active young people. It promotes condom use by associating the use of condoms with behaviour that will earn young people respect from their peers.

There is also support for parents to talk to their children about sex and relationship issues, through the **'Time to Talk'** initiative delivered by Parentline Plus.

It is worth taking a look at them on the internet:

a) http://www.ruthinking.co.uk/

b) http://www.parentlineplus.org.uk/index.php?id=784

c) For 'Want Respect? Use a Condom':
    http://www.youtube.com/watch?v=gGrp2ppsIgo   http://youtube.com/watch?v=0VpX4ZWDviM&feature=related
    http://www.candi.ac.uk/about/news/2006-7/news_%E2%80%9Cwant_respect_wear_a_co.aspx

d) For some American campaigns:
    http://www.teenchoices.com/   (see also "Dating & Marriage")
    http://www.youtube.com/watch?v=Hn6mIK8G2Vc
    (celibate = a person who does not have sex)

Task: Form groups. Each group researches one of the campaigns on the internet and presents them to the class in the next lesson.

© Ernst Klett Sprachen GmbH, Stuttgart 2009 | www.klett.de | Alle Rechte vorbehalten
Von dieser Druckvorlage ist die Vervielfältigung für den eigenen Unterrichtsgebrauch gestattet.
Die Kopiergebühren sind abgegolten.

Kopiervorlage 14:   Evaluating a presentation

	☺	😐	☹	Comment
Do you feel adequately informed about the subject?				
Could you follow the presentation without problems?				
Did the presentation have a clear structure?				
Did the speaker succeed in maintaining your attention?				
Was the language of the presentation adequate?				
Did the speaker explain difficult words or expressions?				
Did he/she speak clearly and loud enough?				
Were the visual aids meaningful and did they support the presentation?				
Were the visual aids clear and legible?				
Did the speaker keep eye contact with the audience?				
How would you evaluate the speaker's body language?				
What is your general impression of the presentation?				

Kopiervorlage 15: Preparing a talk show

The topic

There is a talk show on a British TV channel that deals with the topic of preventing teenage pregnancy.

Organizing the discussion

1.) First choose four experts and a talk show host. The rest of you are people in the audience.

2.) Prepare the discussion. (This needs to be done by everybody!)

2.a) The **experts** need to prepare their arguments:

Expert 1 speaks for the 'RU Thinking' campaign, which is aimed at younger teenagers, promoting messages on delaying first sex and avoiding peer pressure.

Expert 2 speaks for the 'Want Respect? Use a Condom' campaign, which is aimed at sexually active young people. It promotes condom use by associating the use of condoms with behaviour that will earn young people respect from their peers.

Expert 3 speaks for the 'Time to Talk' initiative delivered by Parentline Plus, which offers support for parents to talk to their children about sex and relationship issues.

Expert 4 speaks for 'Teen Choices', an American initiative which promotes no sex until marriage.

2.b) The **talk show host** has to:

- introduce the experts
- ask the experts to make their statements (or to stop speaking)
- lead the discussion
- give a summary of the arguments

2.c) The **audience** has to prepare questions to put to the experts. They should listen carefully while the experts make their statements and then join in the discussion with their questions. They can also bring up new points.

3.) Start the discussion. At the end, when the talk show host has given his/her summary, the audience has to decide whose campaign seems the most promising.

© Ernst Klett Sprachen GmbH, Stuttgart 2009 | www.klett.de | Alle Rechte vorbehalten
Von dieser Druckvorlage ist die Vervielfältigung für den eigenen Unterrichtsgebrauch gestattet.
Die Kopiergebühren sind abgegolten.

Kopiervorlage 16: Useful discussion phrases and tips

For the experts presenting their arguments:

I'd like to begin with …
Next …/Let's turn to …
Another important thing is …
Finally …
I really believe that our campaign is the most
    promising because …
Thank you for your attention.

For the talk show host:

Do we have any questions from the audience?
Yes, sir/madam. What would you like to ask?
Do you have anything to add to that?
I'd like to hear your views on that.
Would anyone like to comment on that?
On the one hand …/on the other hand …

Tips:

> Be well prepared. Take notes of your arguments beforehand.
> Use your notes but speak freely.
> Look at the audience as much as possible.
> Answer people's questions politely.
> Use pictures, diagrams, statistics etc. to support your points.

For everyone:

Expressing opinion:
I strongly believe that …
The way I see it …
In my opinion …
I think …
It's a fact that …

Persuading people:
Surely you see that …
Don't forget that …
You might think differently that …
After all, you must admit that …

Agreeing/disagreeing:
I (don't) agree to …
I am for/against the idea of …
I think it is right/wrong to …
It is (not) true that …
You don't really believe that …

Interrupting/dealing with interruptions:
If I may interrupt here …
I'm sorry, but could I interrupt you there?
I haven't finished what I was saying.
I'm coming to that point later.

Tips:

> Listen carefully to what other people say.
> Try not to interrupt.
> While you are listening, take notes about points you would like to make.
> Ask questions politely.

Kopiervorlage 17: Writing a book review

A book review or a book report is a summary of the book's contents and an evaluation. It aims to inform the readers about what to expect and to give an idea of the wider context (e.g. background information, information about the author etc.).

To prepare your review, you should skim each chapter again, write down headlines for each chapter or larger sections of the book to reduce the contents to the most important facts.

Your review should contain the following aspects:

Bibliographical data:	Author's name, title of the book, place and date of publication, the publisher's name.
	Example: Rai, Bali. *(Un)arranged Marriage*. Stuttgart: Klett, 2007.
	(This is a standard of how to present bibliographical data. Mind the punctuation and italics for the title.)
Classification:	What kind of book is it? (novel, drama, detective story, diary etc.)
Topic:	What is the story about? (no more than one or two sentences)
Summary of the contents:	Give an outline of what happens in the book, the development of the main conflict, its solution and its impact on the characters.
Message:	View the book from a wider context, discuss the problem and relate it to a specific readership. Quote a passage that you find most typical of the book's tone and/or message, most interesting, amusing etc. and explain your choice.
Personal evaluation:	Explain why you like or do not like the book, what it deals with, what is missing, why and to whom you would (not) recommend it etc.

Apart from the bibliographical data, everything must be written in a full text with paragraphs, transitions etc. Your teacher might ask you to include even the bibliographical data in a topic or umbrella sentence.

© Ernst Klett Sprachen GmbH, Stuttgart 2009 | www.klett.de | Alle Rechte vorbehalten
Von dieser Druckvorlage ist die Vervielfältigung für den eigenen Unterrichtsgebrauch gestattet.
Die Kopiergebühren sind abgegolten.

18

Kopiervorlage 18: Film posters of the film *Juno*

© Ernst Klett Sprachen GmbH, Stuttgart 2009 | www.klett.de | Alle Rechte vorbehalten
Von dieser Druckvorlage ist die Vervielfältigung für den eigenen Unterrichtsgebrauch gestattet.
Die Kopiergebühren sind abgegolten.

19.1

Kopiervorlage 19.1:   Film dialogues

Put the dialogues A – I in the order (1. – 9.) that you expect them to appear in the film. While watching, check your answers and take a short note about their context as well as Juno's feelings and the feelings of the other persons involved. Later, explain their context in more detail on an extra sheet of paper (what happens shortly before, what happens in the dialogue, what happens shortly after).

JUNO: I thought I might, you know, nip it in the bud before it gets worse. Because I heard in health class that pregnancy often results in an infant.

BLEEKER: Yeah, typically. That's what happens when our moms and teachers get pregnant.

JUNO: So that's cool with you, then?

BLEEKER: Yeah, wizard, I guess. I mean, do what you think is right.

JUNO: I'm really sorry I had sex with you. I know it wasn't your idea.

A

No.: _____

Feelings: _____

Context: _____

_____

_____

VANESSA: Hi! I'm Vanessa. You must be Juno and Mr. MacGuff. I'm Vanessa.

JUNO: Vanessa, right?

MAC: Hello. Thank you for having me and my irresponsible child over to your home.

VANESSA: Oh no. Thank you. Come on in.

B

No.: _____

Feelings: _____

Context: _____

_____

_____

ULTRASOUND TECH: That's the feet …

ALL THREE: Oooh …

ULTRASOUND TECH: And there's a hand …

C

No.: _____

Feelings: _____

Context: _____

_____

_____

© Ernst Klett Sprachen GmbH, Stuttgart 2009 | www.klett.de | Alle Rechte vorbehalten
Von dieser Druckvorlage ist die Vervielfältigung für den eigenen Unterrichtsgebrauch gestattet.
Die Kopiergebühren sind abgegolten.

19.2

Kopiervorlage 19.2:   Film dialogues

LEAH: Did you hear Bleek is going to prom with Katrina De Voort?

JUNO: Katrina? Pfft, no way. He doesn't like Katrina. It must be a pity date.

D

No.: _____

Feelings: _____

Context: _____

_____

_____

JUNO: Bleeker decided he didn't want to see the baby. Neither did I, really. He didn't feel like ours.

E

No.: _____

Feelings: _____

Context: _____

_____

_____

MARK: I'm leaving Vanessa.

F

No.: _____

Feelings: _____

Context: _____

_____

_____

82

© Ernst Klett Sprachen GmbH, Stuttgart 2009 | www.klett.de | Alle Rechte vorbehalten
Von dieser Druckvorlage ist die Vervielfältigung für den eigenen Unterrichtsgebrauch gestattet.
Die Kopiergebühren sind abgegolten.

Kopiervorlage 19.3: Film dialogues

ROLLO: So what's the prognosis, Fertile Myrtle? Minus or plus?

JUNO: (examining stick) I don't know. It's not … seasoned yet. Wait. Huh. Yeah, there's that pink plus sign again. God, it's unholy.

G

No.: _____

Feelings: _____

Context: _____

_____

_____

JUNO and MARK: (singing together and connecting) Yeah, they really want you … they really want you … and I do, too. (both blush)

(VANESSA appears in the doorwy. Juno immediately puts down the guitar. Mark doesn't notice her immediately.)

H

No.: _____

Feelings: _____

Context: _____

_____

_____

SU-CHIN: Your baby probably has a beating heart, you know. It can feel pain. And it has fingernails.

JUNO: Really? Fingernails?

I

No.: _____

Feelings: _____

Context: _____

_____

_____

Kopiervorlage 20: Film review – „Juno"

Schwanger und Spaß dabei

Warum ernst, wenn's auch heiter geht? Regisseur Jason Reitman hat bereits mit seinem originellen ‚Thank You For Smoking' beweisen, dass seine besondere Spezialität die Zubereitung ernster Sujets in Komödienform ist. Aus der Ausgangssituation von ‚Juno' hätten Kollegen leicht ein Drama backen können: Vorlaute Schülerin wird beim ersten Sex schwanger. Abtreibung kommt nach dem Besuch der dafür zuständigen Klinik nicht mehr in Frage, Mutterschaft ebenfalls nicht, und so entscheidet sich die sechzehnjährige Juno (Ellen Page) dafür, das Kind nach der Geburt zur Adoption freizugeben. Ein reiches Ehepaar aus der Vorstadt ist schnell gefunden. Doch Junos Anwesenheit sorgt bei der zwanghaften Übermutter in spe (Jennifer Garner) und ihrem ins Spießbürgertum hinein gerutschten Gatten (Jason Bateman) für erhebliche Turbulenzen. Reitman hat den Plot mit seinem gefährlich hohen Kitsch-Potential allerdings unter der Zugabe trefflicher Pointen derart gegen den Strich der üblichen Hollywood-Familiendramen gebürstet, dass für Rührung und große Emotionen wenig Raum bleibt. ‚Juno' ist mehr ein Film des sanften Schmunzelns.

Die mittlerweile Oscar prämierte Drehbuchautorin Diablo Cody erzählt keine wirklich neue Geschichte. Aber wie sie die Sorgen und Sehnsüchte des jungen Mädchens thematisiert, ist wirklich ungewöhnlich. Jason Reitman setzt diese rasante, vor Lebenslust sprühende Originalität in Dialog und Wortwitz in entsprechende Bilder um. Die Stärke der Komödie wie die der Titelheldin liegt eindeutig in der spöttischen, staubtrockenhumorigen Alltagsbeobachtung und der sehr genau akzentuierten Charakterzeichnung: der energisch kämpfenden Stiefmutter (Allison Janney), dem verständnisvollen Vater (J.K. Simmons), dem verklemmten, Tic Tac-süchtigen Freund und Kindsvater (Michael Cera). Manche Erkenntnis dürfte genau genommen zu scharfsinnig sein für eine sechzehnjährige Provinz-.Schülerin, doch durch derlei Spitzfindigkeiten sollte man sich den Spaß an ‚Juno' nicht vermiesen lassen. Störend ist da eher die Tatsache, dass Juno auch in Situationen noch eine große Klappe riskiert, in denen etwas leisere Töne passender getroffen hätten. Codys karikaturhaft überzeichnendes Drehbuch bügelt viele einzeln betrachtet spannende Ansätze durch den Zwang zum Bonmot platt und manche Szenen oder auch Nebenfiguren verlieren dadurch schmerzlich an Glaubwürdigkeit.

Kinostart: 20. März 2008 (© www.munichx.de)

Task:

a) Your school has a school magazine in English for which you want to write a review of the film 'Juno', so that your fellow students can decide whether to watch it or not when it is released in the cinemas. At the time of writing you have not been able to watch the film yet, so you take the German review as a model. Sum up the review for your school magazine.

b) Your English penfriend, to whom you always send your articles, knows that you have watched the film by now and wants to know if you agree with the review's opinion about the film or not. Write an email commenting on the review's opinion of the film and why you agree / disagree.

Strategy:

In a *mediation* you do not have to translate word by word. You have to explain the main ideas only. Take notes about the author's basic points first. You should take your notes in English, but in your own words. When writing down the basic ideas of the text, use a different sentence structure and paraphrase ideas from the text.

Kopiervorlage 21.1:

Useful phrases

The ... shot/angle is used to show .../to focus attention on ...

This shot is taken from a high/low angle to show/underline/emphasize ...

The camera is at a great distance from/very close to ...

The perspective achieves a certain effect by ...

The scene/image is shot from ...'s point of view.

It is seen from the perspective of ...

The lighting creates an atmosphere of ...

The character's body language reflects ...

His/her facial expression shows ...

Kopiervorlage 21.2:

Task: Which shots, angles (and movement) would you use for which image?

- raindrops on a window: _____

- couple sitting at a table: _____

- petal of a beautiful flower: _____

- full moon: _____

- boy and girl kissing: _____

- people crossing a street: _____

- a child crying: _____

- a diamond: _____

- an ice skater: _____

- woman on the phone: _____

- neigbours talking over the fence: _____

- happiness: _____

- football that is kicked the whole length of a pitch: _____

22

Kopiervorlage 22:   Camera work

Now, do it yourself: Try to present a person in different moods by using different camera angles and shots. Do not focus on the character's action only. Note: <u>Every</u> member of your group has to be the actor <u>and</u> has to use the camera at least once!

	camera technique	character's action
a shy person		
a happy person		
a sad person		
a frightened person		
a frightening person		

© Ernst Klett Sprachen GmbH, Stuttgart 2009 | www.klett.de | Alle Rechte vorbehalten
Von dieser Druckvorlage ist die Vervielfältigung für den eigenen Unterrichtsgebrauch gestattet.
Die Kopiergebühren sind abgegolten.

Kopiervorlage 23:   Creating your own storyboard

Before a film is shot, a storyboard has to be drawn. (see example storyboard below)

1. Get into groups of four and decide which scenes from the novel "Slam" should be filmed for a trailer.
2. Think of images that represent what you want to show and draw them as sketches into your storyboard.
3. Choose the camera shot, angle and movement that fit best and note them into your storyboard.
4. In the "text"-section write down either what is spoken (if something is spoken) or what happens in the frame.

shot/angle _____

Text _____

_____

shot/angle _____

Text _____

_____

shot/angle _____

Text _____

_____

shot/angle _____

Text _____

_____

shot/angle _____

Text _____

_____

shot/angle _____

Text _____

_____

shot/angle _____

Text _____

_____

shot/angle _____

Text _____

_____

shot/angle _____

Text _____

_____

Klausur A

Creed: „With Arms Wide Open"

Well I just heard the news today
It seems my life is going to change
I closed my eyes, begin to pray
Then tears of joy stream down my face

With arms wide open
Under the sunlight
Welcome to this place
I'll show you everything
With arms wide open
With arms wide open

Well I don't know if I'm ready
To be the man I have to be
I'll take a breath, I'll take her by my side
We stand in awe[1], we've created life

With arms wide open
Under the sunlight
Welcome to this place
I'll show you everything
With arms wide open
Now everything has changed
I'll show you love
I'll show you everything
With arms wide open
With arms wide open
I'll show you everything … oh yeah
With arms wide open … wide open

If I had just one wish
Only one demand
I hope he's not like me
I hope he understands
That he can take this life
And hold it by the hand
And he can greet the world
With arms wide open …

With arms wide open
Under the sunlight
Welcome to this place
I'll show you everything
With arms wide open
Now everything has changed
I'll show you love
I'll show you everything
With arms wide open
With arms wide open
I'll show you everything … oh yeah
With arms wide open … wide open

Tasks:

1. Summarize the thoughts and feelings of the songwriter when he finds out that he is going to be a father and compare them to Sam's thoughts and feelings about fatherhood.

2. After having dinner in the Chinese restaurant (chapter 20), Sam decides to have a last conversation with TH before he takes his poster down.
   Write down what Sam tells TH about what role talking to him and being whizzed into the future has played in his life and why he can finally take his poster down now.

---

[1] awe – a feeling of great respect, sometimes mixed with fear or surprise

Klausur B

Baby-faced boy Alfie Patten is father at 13

By LUCY HAGAN

BOY dad Alfie Patten yesterday admitted he does not know how much nappies cost – but said: "I think it's a lot."

Baby-faced Alfie, who is 13 but looks more like eight, became a father four days ago when his girlfriend Chantelle Steadman gave birth to Maisie Roxanne.

He told how he and Chantelle, 15, decided against an abortion after discovering she was pregnant.

The shy lad, whose voice has not yet broken, said: "I thought it would be good to have a baby.

"I didn't think about how we would afford it. I don't really get pocket money. My dad sometimes gives me £10."

Alfie, who is just 4ft tall, added: "When my mum found out, I thought I was going to get in trouble. We wanted to have the baby but were worried how people would react.

"I didn't know what it would be like to be a dad. I will be good, though, and care for it." […]

Secret

Maisie was conceived after Chantelle and Alfie – just 12 at the time – had a single night of unprotected sex.

They found out about the baby when Chantelle was 12 weeks pregnant.

But they kept it a secret until six weeks later when Chantelle's mum Penny, 38, became suspicious about her weight gain and confronted her.

[…] Chantelle told how she discovered she was expecting after going to her GP with "really bad" stomach pains. She said: "Me and Alfie went. The doctor asked me whether we had sex. I said yes and he said I should do a pregnancy test. He did the test and said I was pregnant. I started crying and didn't know what to do.

"He said I should tell my mum but I was too scared.

"We didn't think we would need help from our parents. You don't really think about that when you find out you are pregnant. You just think your parents will kill you."

But Penny figured out what was going on after buying Chantelle a T-shirt which revealed her swelling tum.

Chantelle admitted she and Alfie – who are both being supported by their parents – would be accused of being grossly irresponsible. She said: "We know we made a mistake but I wouldn't change it now. We will be good loving parents.

"I have started a church course and I am going to do work experience helping other young mums.

"I'll be a great mum and Alfie will be a great dad."

Chantelle and Maisie were released from hospital yesterday. They are living with Penny, Chantelle's jobless dad Steve, 43, and her five brothers in a rented council house in Eastbourne. The family live on benefits. Alfie, who lives on an estate across town with mum Nicola, 43, spends most of his time at the Steadmans' house.

He is allowed to stay overnight and even has a school uniform there so he can go straight to his classes in the morning.

Alfie's dad, who is separated from Nicola, believes the lad is scared deep down.

He said: "Everyone is telling him things and it's going round in his head. It hasn't really dawned on him. He hasn't got a clue of what the baby means and can't explain how he feels. All he knows is mum and dad will help.

"When you mention money his eyes look away. And she is reliant on her mum and dad. It's crazy. They have no idea what lies ahead."

Dennis, who works for a vehicle recovery firm,
75   described Alfie as "a typical 13-year-old boy".
     He said: "He loves computer games, boxing
and Manchester United." Dennis, who has
fathered nine kids, told how he was "gobsmacked"
when he discovered Alfie was to be a dad, too.
80   He said: "When I spoke to him he started
crying. He said it was the first time he'd had sex,
that he didn't know what he was doing and of the
complications that could come."

"I will talk to him again and it will be the birds and
85   the bees talk. Some may say it's too late but he
needs to understand so there is not another baby."

Lovely

Chantelle's mum said: "I told her it was lovely to
90   have the baby but I wish it was in different
circumstances. We have five children already so
it's a big financial responsibility. But we are a
family and will pull together and get through.
     "She's my daughter. I love her and she will
95   *want for nothing." […]*

© The Sun 13 Feb 2009/nisyndication.com

Words:

8   **lad** – boy

8   a boy's **voice is breaking**, when he is changing from a boy into a man

13 **4 ft** (4 feet) = 124 cm

29 **GP** (General Practitioner) doctor

42 **reveal** to show

43 **tum** the lower front part of the body, the stomach

57 **council house** house owned by the government, for which the rent is lower than in a privately owned house

68 **to dawn on sb** to become aware of sth

72 **to be reliant on sb** to be dependent on sb

78 **to be gobsmacked** so shocked you cannot speak

95 **not want for anything** to have all the basic things you need to lead a satisfactory life

Tasks:

1. Summarize the article in about 200 – 250 words.

2. From Sam's point of view, write a letter to Alfie in which you compare your situation to his and in which you give him advice on how to deal with the situation.

© Ernst Klett Sprachen GmbH, Stuttgart 2009 | www.klett.de | Alle Rechte vorbehalten
Von dieser Druckvorlage ist die Vervielfältigung für den eigenen Unterrichtsgebrauch gestattet.
Die Kopiergebühren sind abgegolten.

Rap music blamed for teen pregnancy

By SHAUN BAILEY, Daily Mail

Rap stars are encouraging early sexual activity among teenagers by promoting a degrading view of women, research shows.

Psychologists said their findings from a three-year study presented a worrying picture of how popular music affected the attitudes of boys and girls to sex.

Rap music and hip hop, with their particular emphasis on sex and demeaning depictions of women, were blamed for encouraging early sexual behaviour, leading to the spread of disease and underage pregnancies.

Dr Steven Martino, who led the US study published in the latest edition of the journal 'Pediatrics', said that "sexually degrading lyrics" – many graphic and filled with obscenities – caused changes in adolescents' sexual behaviour.

He said, "These lyrics depict men as sexually insatiable, women as sexual objects, and sexual intercourse as inconsequential. Other songs about sex don't appear to influence youth the same way.

"These portrayals objectify and degrade women in ways that are clear but they do the same to men by depicting them as sex-driven studs. Musicians who use this type of sexual imagery are communicating something very specific about what sexual roles are appropriate, and teenage listeners may act on these messages.

"These lyrics are likely to promote the acceptance of women as sexual objects and men as pursuers of sexual conquest. Despite the fact that degrading sexual lyrics are particularly demeaning for women, they affect adolescent boys and girls similarly."

The same disturbing messages were contained in videos which endorse the portrayal of women as sexual objects, the report said. The research team surveyed 1,461 children aged from 12 to 17 from across the US, asking them about their sexual behaviour and how often they listened to music by various artists including rock, country, rap, blues and pop.

They found that the youngsters listened to an average of 1.5 to 2.5 hours of music a day – not including what they saw on television or videos – but that 40 per cent of the songs referred to sex or romance.

Adolescents who listened to a lot of music containing "objectifying and limiting characterisations of sexuality progressed more quickly in their sexual behaviour" than teenagers who preferred different kinds of music. This was regardless of race or gender, the report said.

The study, called "Exposure to Degrading Versus Non-Degrading Music Lyrics and Sexual Behaviour among Youth," was carried out by the RAND Corporation – a leading healthcare research organisation in the US. It also said that there was a danger that children's opinions about the opposite sex would be affected for the long-term by constant exposure to the lyrics.

Dr Martino added, "It may be that girls who are repeatedly exposed to these messages expect to take a submissive role in their sexual relationships and to be treated with disrespect by their partners.

"These expectations may then have lasting effects on their relationship choices. Boys, on the other hand, may come to interpret reckless male sexual behaviour as 'boys being boys' and dismiss their partners' feelings and welfare as unimportant."

He said that the findings were worrying for teenagers who have more unplanned pregnancies and are more likely to contract sexually transmitted diseases. Increasing rates of sexual activity have serious public health implications. In the US, about 750,000 teenagers become pregnant each year, and an estimated four million contract sexually transmitted diseases.

The study recommended that parents set limits on what music their children buy and listen to. "Censorship is not a solution. But talking to children about music's sexual content can give parents a chance to express their own views, and may prompt teens to think more deeply about the ways in which sex is portrayed – and perhaps distorted – in the music they listen to," Dr Martino said. […]

© Daily Mail 23 August 2006

Words:

1 **to encourage** to give sb confidence to do sth

2 **degrading** causing people to feel that they are worthless

8 **demeaning** causing sb to become less respected

8 **depiction** portrayal

15 **graphic** explicit, clear and powerful

18 **insatiable** (of a desire or need) too great to be satisfied

19 **inconsequential** having no consequences

21 **to objectify** to treat people like tools or toys as if they had no feelings, opinion or rights of their own

23 **stud** a man who is thought to have a lot of sex and who is good at it

30 **pursuer** sb who is chasing sth

30 **conquest** *Eroberung*

34 **disturbing** worrying

35 **to endorse** to support

48 **to progress** to develop in skills

58 **exposure** *Ausgesetztsein*

61 **submissive** describes sb who allows themselves to be controlled by others

65 **reckless** doing sth dangerous and not caring about the risks or the possible results

70 **to contract** to become ill with a disease

72 **implication** responsibility for sth bad that has happened

80 **to prompt** to cause

82 **distorted** changed from its usual meaning, form or shape

Tasks:

1. Summarize the newspaper article below in 150 to 200 words.

2. "Confronting teenagers with sex (e.g. in school education, music, television) just makes them curious to have sex themselves. If we keep sex away from our children, teen pregnancy rates will decrease." Discuss this statement with reference to the text above as well as texts and statistics studied in class.